I Still Cry

by

Cherie Lee

authorHOUSE®

AuthorHouse™
1663 Liberty Drive, Suite 200
Bloomington, IN 47403
www.authorhouse.com
Phone: 1-800-839-8640

First published by AuthorHouse 4/23/2008

ISBN: 978-1-4343-2030-8 (sc)

Printed in the United States of America
Bloomington, Indiana

This book is printed on acid-free paper.

CHAPTER ONE

This story is about a frightened girl named Willa who is unsure of what is going on in her life. She asks questions, such as, "What is happening?" and "Why am I here?" As you read her story, perhaps you can figure it out. It is three o'clock in the morning, and Willa wakes up in a cold sweat. She's scared to death from one of the frequent nightmares that have haunted her since she was a very young child. "Why am I having these horrible nightmares? Why am I so terrified when I wake up?" she asks herself, knowing they are only dreams. They are not consistent with one another. There are more obstacles and other things added to them each time she has one. She doesn't understand what is going on in her head, and no one else seems to have an answer for her.

The bed she is lying on starts spinning around and around, going faster and faster. What is going on? Her first thought was to get out of bed. Her eyes fly open. She sees the walls, and the furniture, but now they're a blur. What is going on? She starts to lose control. All she can do is hang on and hope that she won't fly off and hit a wall. She tries to grab for something to hang onto, but there is nothing. "What happened to the sheets?" Thoughts are reeling in her head.

"They were here not more than a minute ago, when I got into bed."

A minute ago she wasn't spinning either. Her heart is beating very rapidly and she feels as though it will beat right out of her chest. She is terrified; scared that she is going to fall off. Now she's sliding from the bed, which has turned into a large, flat, spinning table. As the table spins, it is also rising up to the ceiling. Will it crush her? Or will she slide off? Which will it be? Which would she rather have? Thoughts are reeling through her brain.

"I don't know!" she cries. "I don't even know how I got here."

There is someone standing beside the table—a man whom she has never seen before. He is staring at her; waiting to grab her as soon as she flies off the table. He wants to take her soul. Somehow she knows what he wants. "How do I know this?" she thinks. "How do I know what this man wants? Have I been here before?" She knows he cannot touch or hurt her while she is on the table, so he keeps pushing and spinning it faster and faster, because there is nothing for her to hold onto. When this all started, she remembers being bound by leather straps, but now they are gone; they just disappeared. With every turn of the wheel, her heart beats faster. She can feel the adrenaline rushing throughout her body, as the heat of her blood intensifies. She can hear the beating in her ears, and sees it pulsating in her chest. Her mouth is dry, and her throat is itchy; making it hard for her to yell for help. As she tries to yell, she starts to choke. All she can do is cry, hoping this will end. She is getting dizzy. Her stomach is now upset and making her nauseated.

"If the spinning doesn't stop soon, I am going to puke!" she screams.

Although her eyes are closed, she can see everything that is going on. Turning her head slowly to the side, she opens her eyes, hoping maybe it will help. She wants all of this madness to stop, and be over. As her eyes open, she can see she is in a large, well-lit, but empty concrete room. The ceiling seems high, but it keeps getting lower as she keeps spinning higher. She can see people standing all around—both inside and outside of the building she is in. Those who are on the outside are trying to get in to help her. Somehow, she knows these people. Even though she can't see their faces, she knows she can trust them. As they see her tears and hear her pleas for help, they try harder to get in. They are pounding on the windows, and she hears the banging and their screams. Their fists are bloody from banging on the windows and the bricks.

"I wish they could help me," she cries.

Not only are the windows too thick to break, but they keep rising higher and higher above their heads.

She can hear herself yelling, "Help me! Please help me! I don't want to be here anymore!"

Those who are inside are dressed in long black gowns with hoods to cover their heads. She cannot see their faces. It's as if they don't have any. All she can see is a dark hole where a face should be and red glowing dots where their eyes should be.

"Who are you?" she cries out to them. "What do you want? Why are you doing this to me?"

No one is listening. Maybe they can't hear, she thought. She knows she is screaming. She can hear herself, but somehow it is all in her imagination. She realizes this because she cannot feel or see her mouth moving. She can only hear her voice.

"Please stop this spinning, Lord! Wake me up! This is only a dream. It has to be. Please don't let it be real. I didn't do anything wrong. I was good. I wasn't bad. Please, God, let it be you who gets me when I fall. I can no longer hold on. If I am doomed to die, I want to go to heaven to be with you. Don't let him get me, whoever he is."

She sobs, feeling the heat of her tears.

"When is this going to end?"

Sobbing out of control, she feels as though she has been here forever with no way out. She is starting to feel weak.

"I cannot hold on much longer. I feel myself sliding off the wheel."

She thinks, "Maybe I'll just die."

As she gives in, everything goes completely dark. Suddenly she feels the sheets. There is now something to hold onto. She grabs them, because the bed is still spinning. She's holding on for her life, allowing herself a little more time to stay alive. Finally, this time, her eyes are really open, and she is no longer dreaming. Now she's awake in her bed.

"I am not dreaming anymore. This is real. I'm awake," she says with a sigh.

She is sweating and hot from the fear, yet she is shivering from what was happening to her in her dream.

"I'm at home safe in my own bed. It was only a dream, but it seemed so real."

She looks around the room making sure this is real. She realizes there is nothing around that she doesn't recognize. The eerie feeling she has afterwards lingers on for days. She doesn't understand what this dream means, or why it keeps coming to haunt her. All she knows is that it is scary and she doesn't want it anymore.

As she comes up from the cellar, feeling someone is watching her, she holds onto the railing. She tries very hard to hurry up the stairs.

She can feel someone watching, and waiting for her to let her guard down, so they can pounce on her and tear out her flesh—eating it while she is still alive. She can't make it up the stairs fast enough. Her heart is pounding faster, and her adrenaline starts to flow; the beating of her heart is pounding in her ears. The further up the stairs she gets, the more there are to climb. They seem to keep increasing with every step she takes. Her legs are burning from the climb, and she feels hands grabbing and scratching her legs; pulling them and making it harder for her to lift them. She is getting tired and winded thinking there is no hope. Finally reaching the top step, she can make a run for the front door, which it is at the other side of the house. As she tries to run through the kitchen, rats and mice are coming at her from the pantry. There is a man sitting there calling her to him.

Without moving his lips, he says, "It's okay, don't worry. I'll take care of you."

"I don't know him, do I?" she thought. Is it grandpa?

"Is that you, grandpa?" she cries.

She cannot see his face. There is a bright light glowing inside the pantry window making it hard to see anything but a big dark shadow. She slowly moves toward him, hoping he is her grandpa. Then he will help her get away from those things trying to grab at her from the cellar, and the rats and mice that are crawling around at her feet. She gets close enough to look at him. He has no face, and there are only two glowing red dots where his eyes should be. She tries to scream but she can't. It feels as though she lost her voice. He is calling her name.

"Willa, come to me. I will take care of you. Willa, I can help you. Come, look into my eyes. You can trust me," he assures her.

He wants her to look into his eyes? What eyes? Why? There are only two red glowing dots where his eyes should be. At this point, she doesn't care who he is, or what he wants. She only wants to get out of the house.

She turns around to run, and then suddenly, the windows in the pantry and the kitchen burst out with glass sprays all over. She has to duck and cover her face to avoid the debris. The wind is blowing so hard it is slowing her down, while the floor beneath her keeps crumbling under her feet. Parts of the floor are soft and mushy—like a big marshmallow. She keeps running, no matter what the impediment may be. She tries as hard as she can to get out of there. As she passes through each room, the windows are flying at her, while the curtains are reaching out to grab her. They are trying to stop her from leaving the house. The wind is blowing so hard she can barely breathe.

"I have to get out of here! He can't have me, whoever he is," she cries.

As she is running, she can see and feel the mice all around her feet, making her stumble as she tries to run. She makes it a point not to look down anymore, because if she does, she will probably stop.

"I can't stop. I've come too far to give up and get caught," she says, sobbing.

The fear of what it is that wants her gives her the courage to keep going. What does that man want? What will happen to me if I stop? She sees herself getting closer to the front door. "Will I finally find protection when I leave the house? Can I get across the street to the church? Will I finally be safe? She is thinking and crying. Where did this church come from anyway? It wasn't there before. It appeared from out of nowhere, but somehow she knew it was going to be there. Fear makes her wonder if it is safe to go into the church since it was never there before.

She can hear footsteps coming closer and closer. Not knowing or caring whose they are, she knows that she can't look back to see who or what it is that is chasing her. She doesn't want to take any chance of slowing herself down. She keeps on running. Finally making it to the front door, she jumps off the porch, trips, and tumbles to the ground.

"I've got to get up!" she cries.

It is hard. She feels as though she can't get up. Suddenly, she is too heavy for her arms, and is unable to push herself back onto her feet. Her head is growing large, making it difficult for her to do anything.

"Lord, please help me! Lift me up!" she sobs.

The ground is turning into mush making it hard for her to extend her arms, for the strength she needs to pull herself up.

Finally, she gets onto her feet, and runs across the street, but now the pavement is getting mushy making it harder to run. It's allowing whatever it is that is chasing her to get closer. She can hear and feel the breath of whatever it is on her neck.

"Don't look back. If you can't see it, then it can't get you. Looking back will only slow you down."

She kept repeating these words to herself. Looking up, she sees a window on the side of the church. A preacher is standing at the altar in front of the pulpit, and a congregation of people are sitting in attendance and listening to his sermon. She screams out for help but no one moves. "They can't hear me," she thought, sobbing uncontrollably. She screamed louder, but again no one heard.

"Just let me get to the church. Someone, will help me?" she cries.

Finally, she gets to the church, but the front door is locked. She tries to turn the handle but it just spins. She pounds on the door.

With an ear-piercing scream, she yells, "Let me in! Please, someone, open the door. There is someone or something out here trying to kill me."

No one came.

The steps are now giving in—crumbling away and leaving a big hole for her to fall into. She hangs onto the door handle, trying to keep her feet as close to her body as possible. Now there are hands reaching out of the hole trying to grab at her, and pull her into the hole.

"Oh, my, God! I am going to die!" she cries.

The doorknob is getting slippery from the sweat of her hands. Her head is spinning and her heart pounding, fearing the worst. Suddenly, not knowing how she got there, she is back on the sidewalk running around the building. She finds an open door and runs inside as fast as she can.

Once inside the church, she runs to the altar. One way or another, she knows it is the only safe place for her to be. The preacher and all the people are gone! What happened to everybody? They all disappeared! It is an abandoned building with broken windows, cobwebs and dust everywhere. She sits down underneath the pulpit with her legs against her chest and lays her head face down on her knees. She is crying harder than before. Her face is wet with tears. She's feeling all alone like she is the only person left in the world. Everyone else is gone. They all just disappeared.

"My doom is here," she sobs.

She feels herself starting to relax, starting to fall asleep, and gasping her breath from all the crying. Just as she starts feeling safe from the evil she was surrounded by, she wakes up to the loud crashing sound of the ceiling and walls falling down around her. Everything is crumbling to the ground. The only thing she can think of doing is to scream out.

"Please, Lord! Help me! Please, save me!"

Her head starts spinning, her heart races, and her throat is dry. She's feeling unbearably helpless, not knowing if she has the strength to keep fighting, and to keep running. This church, she thought, is her only hope. There is nowhere else for her to go. She can't go back to that house.

She hears a voice saying, "There is no one who can save you, Willa. Give up. You are mine, and you have always been mine."

There he is—the man from the pantry. He is standing at the foot of the altar.

"Leave me alone, please! What is it that you want from me?" she cries.

He steps forward, lifts up his right arm and then shoots it out at her—like an arrow coming straight at her. She jumps up screaming, and wakes herself up.

"I'm home in bed. It was just another bad dream."

Turning on the lights, she sits and tries to regain her composure. Her heart is still racing and she is in a cold sweat from the nightmare she just had.

CHAPTER TWO

The House

The house is a duplex; the left side is where Grandpa Carl and Vesta (Grandpa's wife) live. On the right, lives an old woman named Ruby and her two dogs. The front of the house faces west, and the windows on the side of Grandpa's duplex face south. The yards—both front and back—are separated and there is plenty of privacy from the neighbors. The back yard is divided by a six-foot chain link fence that is covered with vines and bushes allowing isolation between the yards. When Willa goes out to play or sit in the back yard alone, she feels as though someone is watching her. It always gives her a scary feeling. Grandpa says she is feeling the stares from the dogs that sometimes poke their noses through the fence. Nevertheless, she still feels the eyes on her neck and it makes her uncomfortable.

As you enter the house at the front door, you walk into a small foyer, and just beyond is the front room. Looking around the room, to the left is a sofa bed, and above it is a picture of Willa's biological Grandmother, Emma, who died before Willa was born. She has always been afraid of that picture, because as you walk anywhere in the room,

Grandma Emma's eyes seem to follow your every move. Directly in front of the foyer is a large archway leading into the living room. Grandpa built shelves on the left side of it from floor to ceiling for Vesta so she could have a place to put her mementos and books. The wall to the right—on the south wall—has a fireplace in the corner, which is close to the living room. Above the fireplace is an elk head (a trophy of Grandpa's). That creepy thing also stares at Willa from everywhere in the room. To the right of the fireplace, along the middle of the wall, sits a console TV/stereo which Grandpa purchased brand new probably in the early 1960s, or maybe late 50s. It has a dark wood cabinet with two doors—the right door houses a thirteen-inch screen TV. The left door houses a record player and AM radio. The front wall, which faces the front yard, has a tall skinny window—the only one in the room. The window is draped in sheer lace curtains. A large armchair sits in front of the window with an end table and a standing lamp on each side of it. On the coffee table in front of the sofa, Vesta lays out her magazines. The ceilings in the house are extremely high. There is a light on the ceiling, and to turn it on, you have to reach up and pull a string that is hanging from it. When you are a small person, that string is beyond reach. Since it is in the middle of the room, Willa can only reach it if she stands on the coffee table—which was not allowed.

As you advance into the house, the next room you enter is the living room. This is the room where Grandpa, Vesta, and visitors spend most of their time. This room has a table model television which sits along the wall dividing the front room and the living room. On that same wall, are pictures of all the grandchildren. The room has a sofa bed against the north wall. Along the east wall sits Grandpa's and Vesta's large winged chairs with a small table and a lamp between them. On the table sits a large ashtray with Grandpa's cigar butts. When Grandpa wasn't at his desk working, or at his workplace, he sat in his chair watching TV and smoking cigars. A large sofa sits in front of the long, skinny window along the south wall. The window has identical sheer lace curtains as in the other room. Willa did not like being in this room because she had to sit on the couch at the north end which was next to the **long dark hallway.** She did not want to sit on that couch at night, because everything was completely dark except for a lamp and the TV in the living room. No matter how many people were in the room, and even when the light was on, Willa still felt the darkness of the **long dark hallway.** There were rules in the house—No one could sit on the floor; absolutely no one could sit on Grandpa's chair; and only the adults could sit on the couch by the window. Willa wished that the couch she had to sit on was in front of the window, so she could feel the sun in the day and not feel the darkness of the hallway at night. The window didn't allow much light into the room, but it let enough sunshine in during the morning and into the evening. The light switch hangs from the tall ceiling with a string to pull, that was again too high up for her to reach.

The long dark hallway—Willa wished that it was never there. It was the scariest place in the house, because no matter what time of day or night, it was always the darkest. The only light in the hallway is a window in the ceiling that was too far up to make a difference. There is no light switch. Entering the long dark hallway, to the right is a door that leads into Grandpa and Vesta's bedroom. This room is off limits to all children, but a couple of times, Willa went in there to sleep because the living room could get a little scary for her and she would have nightmares. In the bedroom is a bed, a dresser, a vanity with a chair, a closet, and a long skinny window with a solid curtain instead of sheers. At the other end of the long dark hallway is the door that leads into the bathroom. That is the room that probably makes Willa hate the **long dark hallway** so much. To enter the bathroom, you have to walk along a small hallway. Along the short hall area is a long closet that is always locked. Vesta said that the closet is most definitely off limits. If anyone should open it, something horribly bad could happen, or at anytime, something just might jump out and get whoever disturbed it. So Willa was terrified every time she walked by the closet to get into the bathroom. It has a toilet with a pull chain, and at the end of the chain, hangs a skinny metal pinecone. Grandpa eventually changed it to a regular toilet—the kind we use today. The bathtub has feet. Willa didn't like it, because anything could be hiding under there, and it was high enough off the ground to see the darkness, but too low, to see anything else that could be underneath it. She always made sure that there was nothing under it at all times when she was in there—especially when she had to go in to take a bath. She thought something could come up from the drain from under the tub and kill her or bite her. She was always thinking about something because the closet was too close to the bathtub, and Vesta said that something horrible could happen to her. A small sink sits in a corner, directly in front of the toilet. The mirror over it is too high, so Grandpa made some steps so Vesta could see into it. Near the ceiling is a small window that is high up, and there's a light with a pull string that had been extended down so little people could reach it. She still had to pass the closet to get to the light switch. Willa made it a point to stay as far from the closet doors as possible. She always tried to walk along the wall opposite of it. The doors were usually locked, but she didn't want to take any chances of accidentally bumping into either of the doors that might upset the 'something' that was in there.

At the other end of the long dark hallway, there is the dining room. It has a built-in bookcase and a sofa bed which is along the wall that is connected to the bathroom. On the southern wall is a makeshift closet which Grandpa made for the clothes no one ever wears. Then there is the long skinny window with sheer curtains, Grandpa's desk, and that was where the phone was. The dining table and chairs are along the wall that goes into the kitchen and it has a light on the ceiling with a string that's too high to reach. Willa was never afraid of this room. This is where she would come to visit Grandpa while he worked at his desk, or talk to her mom on the phone. This room seemed to have the most light in it. From where she sat on the couch, she didn't see the long dark hallway.

The kitchen has lots of light shining in it—more than all the other rooms. It has a large window with the southern light shining through, and the door is wood with a large window on the top half. The refrigerator is the first thing you see as you enter the kitchen. To the right is the stove and then next to it is a water heater. The sink is in the corner at the southern wall, and the window goes from one end of the wall to the other end—it looks like two big squares. Willa did not like being at the sink. She felt too far from anywhere, because there is a door in the kitchen that leads to the cellar. Sometimes when Willa was alone in the kitchen, the door would bang against the kitchen table, which sat in front of it. Grandpa said the winds made the door do that, but in her mind, it was someone or something trying to get out of there. Next to the sink is the washer.

On the other side of the refrigerator is another door that leads into the pantry. The pantry is a large room that stores the dishes, silverware, drinking glasses, food, and lots of other things. It has a window, so it is not dark in the daytime. In addition, the light switch in the pantry is on the wall, which made it easy for her to turn on. Willa did not like the pantry because there were mice playing in there and they made noise during the day and the night.

Willa never liked the cellar, even when she was with Grandpa, her brothers, or cousins. Sometimes she would go with Grandpa down there and wish she never had agreed to go down. It is an ugly, small, concrete room that smells musty like wet cement and wet dirt. The smell sometimes made her lose her breath. Grandpa kept his collections of many things down there and this is where he did his hobbies.

The kitchen door leads to an inside porch, where all the gardening tools are kept, along with a makeshift closet where all the cleaning supplies are kept. Then, walking through the doorway, you come to the back yard. Nothing scary about this house, right? No one else but Willa thinks that this is house is alive.

CHAPTER THREE

The Family

Her name is Willa. For as long as she can remember, she has been going to visit her Grandfather Carl and step-grandmother, Vesta, each and every weekend. She felt good to get away from everybody at home because it was always so crowded with her and her two brothers. Someone was always trying to get individual attention from her mom, Esther. Of all people in the world to get attention, it was not going to be from Esther. She only cared to receive love and always made the children feel guilty for being so needy. Another reason Willa didn't like staying home was because she didn't want to get accused of things she wasn't doing. Although living at home was horrible, she sometimes wished that Friday wouldn't come. She would shiver and wish she could just disappear. If she wasn't there, she wouldn't have to tell anyone how much she hated being at either place.

"Maybe God will grant me my wish someday and give me the power to make myself disappear," she said to herself.

For now she is here, and besides, where would she go? She didn't know anywhere else.

All of Willa's recollections start when she was five years old. Her mother, Esther, was five-foot two and had red hair, but she dyed it brown. She always said that she was dying it back to her natural color. However, when the color faded, her roots were orange. Esther has three children—Ron, Willa, and Serge. She is somewhat round in the belly, and Willa remembers the echoes of Esther's words.

"I never lost the baby fat from any of my pregnancies. If I never had these children, I would still have my figure."

Willa believed that her mom's natural hair color is brown because she and her two brothers have brown hair. Esther likes to pretend she is a meek and caring person when there are visitors around who don't know her very well. In reality, she is very selfish with her love to Willa and her older brother, Ron. She never utters the words, "I Love you!" to them. She has said it many times to their younger brother, Serge. Willa wondered why it was so difficult to say those words to her. Behind closed doors, Esther is an accusing and non-trusting person. She trusted no one, especially the three children, and she made sure they knew it. She is very paranoid, always thinking that one of them is plotting something behind her back. She screams angrily, saying she overheard one of them whispering to another, telling that person something vicious about or toward her. She said she could hear their plans of doing some kind of ungodly act to do to one another. Esther repeated how it is overwhelming for her to raise her three children, even though she wasn't doing it alone. This is why Willa goes to visit Grandpa, so it gives Esther time away from the children—especially Willa. Esther always blamed things on her, even when she knew the boys were the ones causing a ruckus.

Jacob, who is Willa's stepfather, is a short man at five-foot six, and he's chubby. He and Esther met when she was pregnant with Serge. His role in the family is to help Esther raise and discipline the children.

He mostly left the punishments to Esther. It was her job to spank or scold us. Jacob works very hard to give Esther the luxuries she claims to deserve, but on Fridays after work, he goes to the bar to get falling-down drunk. He and Esther would argue the entire weekend and both would get drunk on Saturday. Not one week passed when this did not go on. This is another reason why Willa didn't want to be at home. Jacob treated the three as if they were his own children, and he declared his love to them. However, he made the weekends hell.

Vesta, who is Willa's step-grandmother, hates Willa and her brothers, because Grandpa Carl, when he wasn't out running errands or doing something at work, would spend most of his free time with them. It wasn't the children's fault that he spent all his time with them, but Vesta didn't like it at all. The children didn't spend all that much time with Grandpa, either, because he was either at his work area in the dining room, or sitting in his chair smoking a smelly cigar. Willa didn't understand why Vesta thought that Grandpa Carl gave them more attention that her.

Vesta's words still ring in Willa's ears, "I'm his wife and I am the one who deserves all the attention. Carl is spending more time with you. He is my husband, not yours. Who is the person who slaves for him? Keeps the house clean? For what? So you brats can come over and mess it up? I am the one who does his laundry and all the cooking for him. You kids don't do a thing; all you do is take from him, taking everything that is rightfully mine."

When any of the three would mention to Grandpa Carl what Vesta said, she would deny it.

She would start to cry, and tell Grandpa Carl, "They are just being vindictive little brats. You know they don't like me. They want me out of your life. That way they can have you to themselves. I can't blame them for that. You are such a terrific grandfather. If I were them, I would be jealous, too."

Willa loved her Grandpa Carl very much. She looked up to him, not only because he is tall, but in Willa's mind, he was somehow the most tallest, bravest, and strongest man on the entire earth. He looked to be ten feet tall, but in reality he is six feet tall. To a little person like herself, looking up at him just made him seem taller than everyone else. Grandpa Carl's complexion is olive; his skin is so smooth all the time. He shaves every morning and when Willa was over to visit, he would let her and her brothers stand at his side to watch him shave. It was always fun to watch, especially when he brought his shaving mug out and poured a little water in it. Magic would happen when he put the brush in and stirred it up—lots of lather would foam up. He always took his straight razor and sharpened it on a piece of leather strap that was nailed to the wall. He moved it up one side of the razor and down the other side of the razor. No matter how many times Willa saw him do this routine, she was always amazed. It was different when she watched Jacob shave. It wasn't the same—it was boring. He didn't go through all the preparations that Grandpa Carl had. He just got out a can, shook it, then poured a little of it onto his hands. When he put the stuff on his face, then the foam would appear. That was the only thing she was amused with during his routine—no sharpening of the razor.

Grandpa Carl's hair and eyes are both dark brown. Willa overheard a few women say, "Carl is so very handsome. He is the man we all dream about. Vesta is a very lucky woman to have him." Tall, dark, and handsome, with lots of money—that is the description of Grandpa

Carl. In Willa's mind, he is Prince Charming. He has all the qualities that are described in the books. It made her even more proud of him and that made him a much taller man. Willa wanted to be just like all those women, she thought.

"I want to marry a man just like my Grandpa Carl."

The reasoning behind this was not because of his looks or his money. He works hard for his money, and he is a very proud man. He owns his own concrete company, and always has lots of cash on hand to spend any way he wishes. He is the accountant for his business and his own personal finances. He is the owner and a CPA. Willa remembers him telling her stories about how he struggled to get where he was today. He saved money whenever he could so he could provide a better life and a great future for his children. Someday, he would say, if he was lucky, it would be for his grandchildren also. He wanted to make sure everyone would be provided for.

He said, "It wasn't easy getting to where I am today. It was an uphill battle all the way, but I made it. There is no reason why you kids can't do the same thing. He is a self-made man, that's for sure, and he is very proud of all his accomplishments.

There were times when Grandpa Carl would sit Willa down by his side when he was at his work area in the house. He wanted her to watch and learn how he worked on the books. That way, when she grew older and was no longer in school, she could be the one he would trust to do the books for him and his company. Willa was the only one of the children who seemed to take any interest in the work he does. She never told him how she usually wanted to do something else—something other than to sit by his side learning. She already did a lot of learning at school on the weekdays, but the weekends were her time. She wanted to do something else, something fun, like playing in the yard with the boys or all alone. She never liked all those numbers and accounting is not fun. It is boring and hard, even though the calculator did most of the math work. It was still not fun and she really didn't understand it. She would just pretend to, so she could make Grandpa Carl happy.

Then there were times when Grandpa Carl's work made him mean and angry. It also kept him away from home most of the weekend, leaving Vesta and Willa alone with one another. His absence was mostly due to the fact that he is the owner of the company, and had to go to work on the weekend.

He told us, "I have to go in on the weekends because I hired a bunch of lazy incompetents."

Willa did not like the idea that he wanted her to work, because he didn't show her brothers how to do the work in his ledgers and journals. The main reason for that is because they would always run outside to play.

Grandpa Carl would say, "They are a couple of lazy bums, just like their dad (who by the way is also her dad—a man none of them ever met).

Because they never knew their dad, she couldn't understand why Grandpa would say they were like him. He had no influence on their lives. Esther or Vesta didn't have to sit in his work area to learn how to do the books, nor did they have to work for their living. What makes either of them better than me? She thought. I want to marry a man who will support our children and me. He probably thought that that would make her a better person, but all she wanted was to be a kid. Willa didn't have the guts to tell him she didn't want to work for a living, or that her Prince Charming is going to work and take care of her and their children. She couldn't tell him, for fear that she would get into trouble for having a smart mouth, or worse—wanting to be a lowlife bum. She didn't want him to think of her that way, so time after time she sat there trying to pay attention, and trying not to daydream.

Even though Grandpa Carl is mean, she still loves him very much. He has always been there when she needed him. When the demons in her mind were after her, he was there to comfort and hold her. How could she be mean and tell him how much she hated his job?

Willa's older brother, Ron (who is thirteen months older than her) is tall and skinny. Anyone who knows Grandpa Carl, and saw or met Ron, would say, "He is a miniature version of Carl. He looks just like him." Ron is the darkest of the three children. Their brother, Serge, is short, a little on the chunky side (not fat), and he has a very fair complexion with lots of freckles. Serge is just under Willa in age (thirteen months), and then there is Willawho has always been the smallest of the three (the runt). She has dark brown hair, just like her brothers. Her hair always looks as if someone got a bowl out of the cupboard and put it on top of her head and cut around it. Willa has big round brown eyes. Everyone always complimented the children on their eyes, and her skin is described as light olive. She has always been skinny, and her clothes always had to be altered to fit.

The three of them would be weekend guests at Grandpa Carl's and Vesta's house, but her brothers (everyone called them "The Boys") didn't feel like visiting all the time, so Willa would be stuck going alone. She really wanted to go, because she was bored staying at home with the family. She sees them all week. When she was at Grandpa's, she got the special attention that she craved, and that was definitely something she would not get by staying at home. Was that wrong of her? Is it wrong to want that special attention? Was it her greed that brought her all this grief? She will never know, but it has been her, and not the boys, who can't stop having all these nightmares.

Chapter Four

Willa is five years old. She is very sick and her mom, Esther, figures she has the flu, because of her symptoms. Willa is hot (feverish), and is shivering because she is feeling cold. Her nose is stuffy. She has nausea which is making her too sick to eat or drink anything. Her head hurts so bad that it makes her feel like it is going to blow up. She is also having a hard time breathing. Grandpa Carl, however, is a very determined man. Once he has his mind set on something, he goes after it and usually succeeds in getting his way. He wanted to take Willa for the weekend and he was going to, no matter what the circumstances were. He assured Esther that he would take Willa to see his doctor.

He said, "I'll pay the doctor's fee, and buy any medicine that may be prescribed for her. Let me do it. I can afford to do this more than you can since you have a houseful of mouths to feed. What do you say?"

"Who can argue with that logic?" Esther said.

Grandpa Carl is a man of his word; he did take Willa to the doctor. The doctor he took her to was in Walsenburg, Colorado. They live in

Denver and that's a long way to go just to see a doctor. Before they set out on their journey, Grandpa Carl and Vesta made the back seat of the car as comfortable as possible for her. Grandpa also put a bucket with a couple of trashcan liners there just in case she got sick anytime during the trip. Vesta gave her some Pepto-Bismol for precautions.

She said, "I am not in the mood to hear anybody puke."

The ride was cold; there was lots of snow all around, on the ground and falling from the sky. As Willa lay in the back seat, bundled in warm clothes, and wrapped in a blanket, she stared out the back window at the falling snowflakes. They became hypnotic to her, and put her in some sort of a trance. She was asleep during most of the trip. When they left her house that morning at seven o'clock, everything seemed so grey and bleak. However, when they arrived in Walsenburg, it was noon and the sun was shining bright with the fresh snow on the ground. Willa thought it was a different day when she woke up. Grandpa blamed the bad weather for them arriving a half hour later than expected. When they got there, Grandpa pulled into the parking lot of a motel, and went in to rent a room for the night. They all went into the room and Grandpa called the doctor.

"Is it too late to see my granddaughter, Willa?" he asked. "Okay, we will be right over."

Then he hung up.

"Come on, let's go; he will wait for us to get there," he said in a rushed tone.

They all got in the car and drove the couple of blocks to the doctor's office.

Willa was afraid. Not only was this a strange town where she had never been, but she didn't even know the man who was getting ready to examine her. Vesta stayed in the room with her, because she was crying and didn't want to be alone.

"Don't let him touch me, please!" she cried.

As he put the stethoscope to her chest, she started screaming, so Grandpa had to come into the room to calm her down. The doctor listened to her chest, made her open her mouth, and felt her throat. Willa was squirming all along, because she didn't want to be there. DIAGNOSIS: Pneumonia.

"How could that be? It came on so quickly. Her mom said she was fine yesterday. She was running around and playing in the snow with her brothers," Grandpa explained to the doctor.

"She could have had it for a couple of days, maybe even a week, without knowing because the fever didn't hit her until last night, right?" the doctor asked.

Then he turned and looked at Willa.

"Have you been feeling sick the last couple of days?" he asked.

Willa nodded her head, yes, and said, "But I was only throwing up. Mommy said it was because I made a pig of myself, and probably over ate something. I like to eat a lot of peaches," she explained.

He then turned to Grandpa and said, "See, it started a couple of days ago. It did give a warning, but sometimes the warning signs are hard to detect, especially in little girls who like to eat lots of peaches."

They all laughed.

The conversation quickly changed, and everyone got serious.

"I want to keep her in the hospital for observation. We need to get oxygen into those lungs of hers," he said seriously.

Willa started to cry again, "I don't want to go to the hospital. Please don't make me go. I'll be good. I won't throw up anymore. Please, can I go back home now? I'm not sick anymore. Please, don't make me stay," she begged, as she clung to Grandpa.

"It's not as bad as you may think it is. Do you know what a hospital is?" the doctor asked.

She shook her head, "No."

She really didn't know what a hospital was, but it didn't sound good. She revealed that she knew that she and her brothers were born at one, and one time, Jacob's Aunt Sarah went to one and she died.

"I don't want to go there. I am already born, so now that means I am gonna die. I don't want to die," she cried.

"No, those are not the only reasons people go to the hospital. Sometimes when we get sick, we need special attention to get better quicker. Nurses can give you the special attention you need for your condition. This is to help you feel better, so you can go home and have fun, instead of going home and staying in bed because you are too sick to play. Do you understand what I am trying to explain to you?" the doctor calmly asked.

She looked up at Grandpa; he nodded his head "YES," to assure her, everything the doctor just said was correct.

"Doctor Rivers made a special trip just for you. Today is his day off, but he came to see you. I think you owe him the courtesy of doing what he says," Grandpa Carl told her.

"Okay, I'm sorry for what I said, and I'm sorry for the trouble I've caused you," she apologized.

When the doctor was finished talking to Grandpa Carl, Vesta and Willa, a nurse came into the exam room.

She looked at Vesta and Willa, and told them, "You can go to the lobby and wait, while Mr. Lopez signs the admittance papers."

They got up and went to the lobby to sit. Grandpa Carl returned to sit with us. A nurse came out to the lobby with a wheelchair. Willa started crying again.

"Don't worry, Willa. Everything is going to be okay. My name is Elsie, and I'm the nurse who is going to be with you most of the time you are here," she assured her.

Elsie turned and looked at Grandpa and Vesta, and asked them, "Have you eaten lunch yet?"

"No, as a matter of fact we haven't. We went directly to the doctor's office when we got into town," Grandpa Carl explained.

"I have to take her vital signs and get her situated in her room. You are more then welcome to come back in about an hour after you have lunch. Our policy states there are no visitors until we get the patient situated. I apologize for any inconvenience," she told them.

"No problem." Grandpa said. "We need to get settled ourselves."

Then they looked at Willa and Grandpa said, "Now you be good. Elsie is going to take care of you. We are going to eat and then get unpacked. We'll be back in about an hour."

"Okay."

"There's a café on Main Street, just a couple of blocks away, and they have really good food there," Elsie told Grandpa Carl.

Willa cried as they said their goodbyes. She watched Grandpa and Vesta leaving the hospital. While Willa was being wheeled to her room, she kept staring at them leaving. She made sure her eyes were on them at all times until they disappeared from her sight. Elsie pushed the wheelchair into the elevator and they went up to the floor to where her room was.

"Okay, here we are. This is the room where you will be spending the night," she explained. "Is Mr. Lopez your father or your grandfather?" she asked.

"He's my grandfather," she told her.

"Why did he bring you to the hospital instead of your parents?" she asked Willa.

Willa told her, "Because my mother is at home taking care of Ron and Serge and she couldn't come all the way out here."

"Where do you live? Do you not live in Walsenburg?" Elsie asked.

"No, I live at home, with my mom, Jacob, Ron, and Serge."

She didn't know if she was asking all those questions to be nosy or if she was trying to be nice and break the ice between the two of them. If she was trying for the latter, it sure did work, Willa felt more comfortable now. Elsie looks like a Barbie doll dressed in a nurse's uniform. She is really nice. Willa really liked her a lot. She is tender, loving and caring. She explained to her everything that was in the room, and what each individual thing did. Willa kept asking questions about it all. She was so fascinated by everything. It was all new to her and very scary. The bed was set up with a plastic tent at the front end where the pillow was, and where she would lay her head.

"How come that plastic is over the pillow? Isn't that a dangerous place? My mom told me not to put plastic over my head because I could suffercate and die," Willa exclaimed.

"No!" Elsie said. "First of all, the word is suffocate, not suffercate, and second, the plastic that is on this bed, is a tent that is filled with oxygen. It will help you to breathe better. Here, stick your arm inside and feel the air coming out of it," Elsie said.

Willa put her arm in and was amazed. There really is air inside. Elise showed her the plastic tube that went from the tent to the oxygen tank. Elsie then helped her out of her clothes, and put her into a hospital gown. Willa was eating lunch when her grandpa and Vesta came back.

"Hi! How are you doing? Looks like you're feeling more comfortable now. You look a lot calmer then you did when we saw you earlier," Grandpa Carl said.

"Yes! I am. I don't feel so scared, and Elsie is really nice to me. She told me I have to eat this soup; she calls it broth. She said it's okay if I throw up, but she doesn't think I will because she gave me some yucky stuff that I had to drink. She was standing beside me to make sure I drank it all down, because it's important."

She rattled on about everything she and Elsie talked about.

"We brought you some gifts; something to keep you occupied, just in case you get bored. We are only allowed to stay here an hour, but we can come back after supper to visit for another hour," Grandpa Carl assured her.

"How come you have to keep leaving? I don't want to be here alone. Why can't you stay here with me?"

Willa started to cry again.

"I thought you were feeling more comfortable here. What's wrong?" Grandpa asked.

"I miss you and I want to go home now. I feel much better. See, I can breathe better now."

"Yes, you can breathe better now because you are underneath the tent that has oxygen going through it," Grandpa Carl said.

Willa opened up the presents they bought her.

"My favorite, how did you know to get me a Mickey Mouse coloring book? I also like Raggedy Ann. You got my favorite things. Thank you both very much."

Willa gave a big smile and hugged both of them. That took her mind off of her situation for a while. In her mind, the stay at the hospital wasn't going to be so bad after all. The only scary parts were being all alone in a strange place. Elsie came in and colored in her books with her until it was time to go to sleep. The night came and went. It was no big deal anymore. She remembers getting back to Grandpa Carl's house. That day (she didn't know if it was a weekend or a weekday), she stared at the sky. It was cold and very bright outside, but even though it was bright, somehow the sky over Grandpa's house looked gray. It's in the dead of winter, sometime around January, because Christmas was past and that is her most favorite time of the year. Living in Denver, January is not warm and is usually snowy and very icy. Willa was feeling scared that day for some unknown reason. She had never felt this fear within herself before, or maybe she had, and was too young to remember it. That was the day when the terror started in her head, and which has stayed with her, which seems like a lifetime. That night she woke up screaming because she was having nightmares about a man calling her into the pantry, in the house where her Grandpa lived. He was telling her that the rats and mice were going to get her and tear her to pieces if she didn't come to him. She tried to run away from him, when suddenly she saw and felt her head—it was growing bigger and bigger like a balloon. It seemed as though it would soon explode. There was also an odor—a gross smell, and something she has never experienced smelling before. The smell was making her sick to her stomach, all the while, her body seemed to be too tiny to move—too small for her head. She could see the mice; they started to crawl on her hair, climbing up to gnaw on her face, and to make it explode. Willa woke up screaming for Grandpa to come help her. Willa's screams kept getting louder each time, giving it about a second of rest between the screams. She was shivering so fiercely from the nightmare. Grandpa Carl came running to her rescue.

"What's wrong?" he asked. "Why are you screaming like this? What happened?" he asked again.

"I had a bad dream. It was so scary, but it seemed so real," Willa cried.

She told grandpa what happened in the dream. He took her into his and Vesta's bedroom, and put her to sleep between them that night. Since then, that horrible night, Willa started having bad dreams (nightmares) and bad experiences in that house. These experiences felt like they would stay with her forever.

Chapter Five

All three children were visiting one weekend (Willa was about six years old). They were being normal, active, and bored kids. They were jumping around in the living room, wrestling and playing, "Cowboys and Indians." Esther made sure to send pants for Willa to wear on the weekend, to play in, so she would not ruin her dresses. Vesta was yelling at them to settle down or else they would get themselves into a lot of trouble. They are kids. They paid no attention to her warnings. Around Vesta's third warning, they went to play by the window, since it was on the other side of the room. They figured if Vesta couldn't see them, that she couldn't hear them either. They finished watching the Saturday morning cartoons. What else did she expect them to do? There was nothing else on TV—at least nothing that would interest them. They tried to be quiet, but their laughter got louder each time they were warned.

Vesta was yelling, "Behave yourselves; the three of you better settle down. I am not going to tell you again. If I hear any more commotion, I am going to be forced to tell your grandfather that you are all being bad, and not one of you is listening to a word I say. You don't want me to do that, do you?" she screamed.

"NO!" they all said together. "We'll behave!"

"But what else is there to do?" Ron asked.

"Can we go outside to play?" Willa asked.

"No! Absolutely not. You know better than that. It is too cold and windy out. Your grandpa would have a fit if he found out you kids went outside to play. I am sure the three of you can find something quiet to do."

This went on a few more times and their hard-headedness stayed with them. They were bored and restless. They couldn't go out to play in the back yard because it was snowing and the wind was blowing, making it even colder.

They had been playing "Cowboys and Indians" when they heard a noise in the dining room—a noise that sounded like a loud crash of glass breaking. They looked at each other.

"What was that?" Serge asked.

"I don't know," said Ron. "Let's go see what it was."

Since Ron is the oldest, they always agreed to whatever he suggested. The three of them got up to look down the long dark hallway to see what it was. The three went creeping slowly to the other side of the room because they didn't want to get into trouble for being nosy, and not minding their own business.

"Vesta is probably drinking and dropped some glasses," Ron giggled.

"Yeah, she probably slipped on something she spilled, while she was drinking her whiskey and dropped all of the glasses," Willa said, giggling.

They started laughing quietly, so Vesta wouldn't get mad at them for laughing at her. They got to the couch and then peeked down the hallway. They all thought they would see Vesta bent over picking up broken glass. Oh, my, God! None of them were expecting to see what they saw. Well, they did know what it was that they expected to see, and this was not it. There, at the end of the hallway, in the dining room was a hideous sight. Something the three of them saw, not only Willa, but her brothers, too. She wasn't dreaming this time. There, at the end of the hallway, was a devil. He was huge and red with the body of a naked werewolf; the eyes were bloodshot. He was staring at them. He used his long finger, which had long black fingernails to wave at them and to lure them to him. He called them by their names.

"Come here, Ron; come to me, you and your sister, Willa, and your brother, Serge," he said, with blood dripping out of his mouth and onto the floor. "Come to me. You wouldn't listen to your grandmother, and you kept jumping around, making all kinds of noises, calling me to come get you. Well, I am here now. I am here to take you all with me, just like you wanted. I like to eat the skin off of bad children's bones, and suck out their souls and eat their juicy pounding hearts."

He was laughing. They were shocked. They were staring open-mouthed at him. Willa didn't know about her brothers' feelings at that time, but she was terrified. The devil started walking toward them. He stepped into the long dark hallway to come for them. They all jumped onto the couch, burying their faces into it. They started crying and screaming. Willa began to panic. She could hear her heart beating loudly and was wondering if anyone or anything else could hear it. Maybe if he could hear it, it would sound juicier to him and he would come to her and eat her while she is still alive.

Willa had a theory. She thought if she couldn't see something or someone, then it or they couldn't see her. So she tried to bury her head deeper into the cushions and pillows.

"Don't let him get me or my brothers, please!" She prayed in silence. "I promise I'll never be bad again. I will listen next time. I will be better. Please, help save us, God!"

Willa remembered a prayer Grandpa had taught her when she was sick and was having nightmares. So she started chanting the prayer out loud, repeatedly.

"Now I lay me down to sleep. I pray the Lord my soul to keep. If I should die before I wake, I pray the Lord my soul to take."

It felt as though the devil was getting closer. Willa could feel the blood rushing through her veins, making her feel warmer inside. She could feel the hair on the back of her neck standing up.

"What's happening?" she thought.

She didn't want to look up to see, because if he was still there, then she would expose herself to him. Suddenly, it was very quiet. The only sounds she could hear were the whimpering and sniffles from her brothers and herself. The quiet made her skin crawl, and the expectation of what may happen seemed forever. Then suddenly she heard footsteps coming at them through the hallway.

"Oh, no!" she thought. "Here it comes!"

She kept crying and praying silently. She was so afraid; she tensed up preparing herself for whatever was to happen to her.

The footsteps got closer and then suddenly they stopped. It was Vesta. She came running from the kitchen (where she had been cooking), to see what was going on. She heard the three of them shrieking.

She told them, "One minute, the three of you were laughing and then the next minute, you were all crying and screaming. What's going on in here?" she asked.

They told her about the devil standing at the end of the long dark hallway and how he was calling them to him and walking toward them; he even knew their names.

"There was a devil standing in the hallway," Ron told her, his voice was still shaky from the scare. "We heard glass breaking, and we went to see what happened, to see if you were okay. There he was standing in the dining room," he explained.

"Yeah," Willa interrupted. "He called us, and he knew our names."

Vesta told them that it was just their imagination. She said they probably felt guilty about jumping around and not listening to her; when they should have been playing in a nice settled manner.

"First of all," Vesta said, "I warned you before now that you have to deal with your own conscience, and second, you kids are crazy! What glass are you talking about? There is no glass on the floor, and I didn't hear any glass breaking. Besides, how do you know if it was the devil or not? Have you actually seen what the devil looks like?" she questioned.

"Yes, we have. We've seen pictures and we also saw movies with him in it, but this one was scarier than any of the ones we've ever seen before, because he was real," Ron told her.

"Okay, that's enough of this foolishness. Your grandpa can deal with it when he gets home," she said.

It was left at that.

When Vesta went back into the kitchen to finish cooking, the three of them sat still and very quiet. They looked at the TV, and didn't even care what was on. Willa couldn't help looking all around the room, noticing that not only was she doing it, but Ron and Serge were doing it, too. All she could think of was to keep her concentration away from looking into the long dark hallway. It seemed so much harder not to look into it when she was trying so hard not to. They finally started to pay attention to the TV since there was a funny movie on. They were all glad of that—finally something to make them laugh. Their laughs were as quiet as could be—for fear of what may happen if they got loud. They were also afraid to talk to each other, because if they made any noise, the devil might come back to claim their souls and their juicy beating hearts.

When their grandpa came home that evening, they all told him what had happened. Naturally, Vesta told him about their misbehaving, which meant he believed her story and not theirs. He said they made up these tales to keep themselves from getting into trouble. Whenever any of the incidents happened, their grandpa was usually away at the store, doing some kind of errand or at work. Vesta was always in the kitchen cooking.

Willa promised to be better and that was a promise she intended to keep. That was the scariest experience she had been through and she didn't want it to happen again. She never knew that when kids were making lots of noise, while playing and having fun in the house, it meant they were calling the devil to them. Well, she knows now, because he told them. Her promise to herself was, "I'll stay as still and as quiet as I can, from now on."

CHAPTER SIX

One weekend in the summer, when Willa was still six years old, she was the only one who went to spend the weekend at her grandpa's house. Grandpa's next-door neighbor, Ruby, asked her to come over to visit. For some reason, Willa never felt comfortable at Ruby's house. She didn't even feel comfortable being around her, even though Ruby was extremely nice to her all the time. Maybe it was because of her dogs. They were both huge German shepherds. They are attack dogs and trained to attack on command. Willa never felt comfortable with the dogs, because they would stare at her through the fence and bushes that separated their two back yards. She had a dream once that she was playing in the back yard by herself, when the two dogs jumped over the fence and came chasing after her. She tried to run into the house but they caught her. They ripped her clothes and bit her skin, making her blood gush out. Ruby was just standing and looking over the fence at what was happening. She didn't even call the dogs back.

Willa may have felt uncomfortable because of Ruby's age; she was about eighty years old, very wrinkled, and skinny. She reminded her of a storybook witch. She had long white hair which was always wrapped in a bun on top of her head. But there were a couple of times when Willa saw her hair down and it was very long—down to her waist or maybe even longer. This wasn't the first time Ruby had ever invited Willa over for a visit. She had been to her house before, but not to visit. Willa knew her imagination liked to tell her things that were not true, but she didn't want to be too trusting. She went to visit Ruby anyway, against her bad feelings. She didn't want to hurt her feelings. Also, she didn't want to be bored and alone with Vesta either. She couldn't help but think that Ruby only wanted her over to toss her into her oven and eat her for dinner. "No!" she thought, it is only my imagination. I need to stop thinking that.

They sat and talked for a long while. Willa actually started to feel more comfortable with Ruby and her house. The ugly thoughts about her being a witch were all gone. They talked about different things, mostly about when Ruby was Willa's age and how her mother had made her go to dancing school. As she got older, she went to modeling school and became a model (she didn't look like any model Willa had ever seen). Ruby would take out photo albums and show them to Willa. You would never have thought that that old woman sitting there was the same person in those albums. They also played old maid. Meanwhile, the time was passing so quickly because they were actually having fun together, and enjoying one another's company. As time went on, they both got thirsty, so Ruby went to the kitchen to make some tea. Willa waited patiently, feeling all alone and scared. She was feeling as though she was waiting forever. Ruby was taking a long time to come back and the house was getting spookier, because it was starting to get late and she could hear the teakettle whistling. Vesta had told me that I had to be home by five o'clock to eat supper, she thought.

"I don't know what time it is!"

The dogs suddenly started barking and howling in the back yard. What if she is letting the dogs in to eat me while she stands and watches them do it? she thought. Willa started to get more scared than she was already; hearing the whistle of the teakettle and the barking and howling of the dogs was getting almost too much to take.

She got up and started calling for Ruby. She wondered what was taking her so long. By this time, Willa was really feeling uncomfortable. She was afraid to go through Ruby's long dark hallway to look for her. (Since she is afraid of the one at Grandpa's house, she is certainly more afraid of this one because she doesn't know what to expect, in this house.)

"Ruby!" she yelled. "I'm still in here waiting for you."

Ruby didn't answer. "Why isn't she answering?" Willa thought. "Where could she be? Why is she taking so long?" Questions were reeling all around in her head. Willa got up and started walking very slowly down the long dark hallway toward the kitchen. She was afraid of something or someone reaching out to grab at her from either the bedroom or the bathroom. There wasn't any other way to go check on Ruby. She had to pass those rooms to get to the kitchen.

"Please, Ruby," she yelled. "Please, come to me so I don't have to go all that way. Let me know you're okay," she yelled.

There was no response from Ruby. The dog barks and howls were getting louder; the whistle of the teapot was a constant ringing in her ears, and made it harder to take the journey to the kitchen. She slowly crept through the hallway, keeping her guard up, and looking all around her at all times. She made sure not to look into the doorway of the rooms, just in case anything would try to come charging at her. "What if the dogs came running at me? What would I do then? Would I be safe jumping into the bedroom or the bathroom?" she thought. She didn't know what to think at this point. "Maybe I should just turn around and run out the front door, and just go home to Grandpa's house."

When she finally reached the kitchen, she saw Ruby lying on the floor. There was blood coming from her head.

"Oh, my, God! What happened?" she screamed.

She could hear the dogs jumping up at the back door trying to get in. The only thing she could think of doing at that point was to turn around and run for the front door.

"I need to get out of this house, before whatever or whoever did this to Ruby has a chance to do the same thing to me."

She was crying hysterically, and started running through the dining room. She ran down the hallway through the living room, and then into the front room. It seemed to be taking forever to get to the door. She never imagined in her wildest of dreams how far it really was to get there. She felt like she had weights on her feet. It seemed to be taking forever to get out, or at least to the front door. The tears she was crying were clouding her eyes, making it hard to see. Willa couldn't seem to run fast enough, because there were eyes staring at her from all over the place—piercing through to her soul. They were trying to keep her in this house to do to her what they had done to poor Ruby. Willa could hear breathing and could feel the breath on the back of her neck.

"Maybe it's the dogs. Maybe they got into the house and they are chasing me. Why can't I get to the front door any faster?" Her thoughts were scattered. She felt herself trying to catch her breath while the hot tears were pouring down her cheeks.

When she finally reached the front door, she grabbed for the doorknob thinking, "Finally, I can get out of this house." She tried to open the door. "Oh, God! No!" she thought. "I can't do it. It won't open for me." The knob was just spinning.

Willa screamed, "Please, God, help me. Get me out of here! Get me out of this house! Somebody help me!" she yelled.

Finally, she was able to get the door opened. She ran out of the house, hearing the screen door slam behind her.

"I'm out!" she thought. She ran next door, tripping over her feet; she couldn't get there fast enough. She was screaming because she was not only terrified from what she had just seen and experienced, but the shock was too much for her. Grandpa heard the screaming, and grabbed her up into his arms and held her. He was trying to calm her down, and trying to find out what had happened. He wanted to know why she was crying. She couldn't get any words out. She wanted to tell him that Ruby was dead and whatever or whoever is in her house, killed her and was trying to do the same to her. No matter how hard she tried, she just couldn't get any words out. She couldn't stop shaking and crying. Her heart wouldn't slow its beat. She could barely catch her breath.

The only thing she could do was chant over and over, "Ruby."

Grandpa and Vesta were trying to decide which one of them would have to go next door to find out from Ruby what had happened. Willa clung to Grandpa.

"Please, don't leave me! Don't let go of me!" she begged. "They might get you, too, or what if they followed me here? Don't leave me alone, please!" she sobbed.

Her pleas and Ruby's name were the only ones that could come out of her mouth.

Vesta decided she would go next door to talk to Ruby, and ask her what had happened, since they couldn't get anything that made any sense out of Willa. When she returned, she was pale and crying.

She told Grandpa, "Go call the ambulance. Ruby is lying in a pool of blood on the kitchen floor."

Willa cried harder, feeling her face hot with all the tears. The memory of what she saw in Ruby's kitchen kept playing on and on in her head. Willa couldn't believe it. All her nightmares were real. Evil was stalking, and taking the souls of innocent people. Look what happened to Ruby. "I hope she didn't hurt," Willa thought. "I wonder if she is hurting now." Willa started praying for Ruby's soul.

"Dear God, this is Willa. I am asking that you take Ruby's soul, so she won't hurt anymore. Please don't let them keep it. Don't let her feel the pain. Thank you, God."

Grandpa got up and went to the dining room where the phone was.

"What did you do to her?" Vesta yelled.

"I didn't do it, they did it." Willa cried.

"Who did it? Was there someone else in the house besides you?" she asked.

"I don't know. I didn't see anybody. She just got up to go make some tea for us, because we were thirsty. She was taking too long, so I called her, and she didn't answer. I went to see what was taking her so long and I saw her like that," she cried, still shaking and shivering from the horror.

When the paramedics arrived, Grandpa went into Ruby's house with them. Willa watched as they took Ruby out on a stretcher and put her into the ambulance. They took her to the hospital.

"Maybe the doctors can help her?" she asked, looking up at Vesta. "Maybe?"

"We'll see," Vesta replied.

The next day, Grandpa called the hospital to find out how Ruby was doing, and about her condition. They informed him that Ruby had a stroke and fell; she hit her head on the edge of the stove when she fell, and she died instantly."

No one had killed her, not Willa or any unseen monsters conjured up in her head. Ruby once told her that she didn't have any living relatives. The only family she had was the two dogs. Willa still couldn't figure out how one minute Ruby was fine, and then the next minute, she was dead. Not a word; no warning or anything else. Didn't she know? Did she feel anything before going into the kitchen? Willa wished she had the answers to her silent questions.

CHAPTER SEVEN

When Willa was seven, her brothers stopped going over to visit Grandpa's house on the weekends. They didn't go over as much anymore, which meant she was the only one there with Vesta. The reason they slowed their visits is because Vesta hated them so much that she would say and do anything to get them into trouble with Grandpa. While Grandpa was away, Vesta would think up lies to tell him about the kids. Sometimes Willa wondered where Vesta got the time to make up these little stories, since she was supposedly always busy doing something, mostly in the kitchen.

When Grandpa would return home from wherever he was, Vesta would be in hysterics; she was a completely different person than she was not less than a minute before she saw Grandpa. Vesta would start shaking and crying, telling him lies that would get him furious at the kids. She told him stories about how the boys and Willa got into her garden and trampled her favorite flowers—when all along she was the one who did it, not the kids. She would go outside to work in her garden, and then every once in a while—for no reason at all—she would start pulling out the flowers and crushing them. There were a few times also when she would get mad for whatever reason unknown to them, and slam the back door hard, breaking the window; then she put the blame on the kids. She would tell him, "They were running in and out of the house and slamming the door behind them. I tried to warn them not to be doing that. I tried to tell them what might happen, but they kept right on doing it—not listening to a word I said, or any of my warnings. I tried to warn them several times. I just don't know what to do to please them anymore. I am fed up!" she would cry.

She would stand there in front of them telling these lies. It was if they weren't around.

Vesta would do stupid childish things, just for the fun of it; that way she could put the blame on any or all three of the children. It would depend on her mood, or whom she was the most angry at. Willa figured out why these stories were invented. Vesta made them up when she was getting drunk. It was her suit of armor, and her protection of sorts. She knew Grandpa didn't like her to drink, and so making up lies about the children helped her to hide her drinking. This way it kept Grandpa away from her so he wouldn't smell the liquor on her breath. If he knew she had been drinking and was the one who was doing the things she accused the kids of doing, he would beat her up. No, Vesta wasn't stupid. She only did stupid things. Willa thought that in Vesta's mind she must have thought it was better to blame the children for doing the things she did. That way, they were the ones to get hit for it instead of her. Willa could only speculate why Vesta did and said those things. That was the only reason she could think of as to why she would be so cruel to make up the lies she did. Did Vesta think the kids didn't feel the pain of the spankings? Willa wanted to question her, but never did, for fear of what might happen to her—and most of all her brothers, for her having a smart mouth.

Grandpa would ask, "Why are you kids acting so rebellious toward Vesta? Why can't you respect our home and our belongings? Why are you so destructive? Do you have so much hate for Vesta that you can't even respect our possessions?" he would yell, shaking and glaring at them angrily.

There was no telling the truth in that house. When they tried to tell him that Vesta was lying, he would not believe anything they had to say.

His response to them was, "It's a sin to lie. You can go to hell for it. Do you want to go to hell? Do you want the devil to take your soul? You will burn for eternity in the fires of hell. Is this what you want?"

NO!" they replied, hanging their heads and crying, too afraid to look up at him.

If any of them said one word in retaliation to the story, Grandpa would beat Ron and Serge with an open hand and then with his fists. When they fell to the ground, and were all curled on the floor, he would start to kick them.

They would cry and scream out to him, begging, "No more, Grandpa, please! I'm sorry for what we did. It won't happen again, I promise, please stop."

They didn't have anything to be sorry for, because they didn't do any of the things Vesta had accused them of doing. They had nothing to do with those lies that were made up by Vesta. Curling up in the fetal position was their only way of salvation for their small bodies. Willa guessed that it helped, and there were never any broken bones after all was said and done.

During all the rage and fury, Willa vividly remembers sitting all alone in the corner of the room watching her brothers get beaten. There was nothing she or anyone else could do about it, once it started. She wished she could help them. She wished that more than anything else, but if she did something she might have gotten beaten along with her brothers. So each time it happened, she curled in the corner of whatever room they happened to be in, and tried not to watch. She thought that maybe if she couldn't see what was going on, it really wasn't happening and that would mean it was all a bad dream. Just like all the other bad dreams, she had been having. No! It's not a bad dream. It is really happening. How else was she able to hear the cries and the pleadings of her brothers begging Grandpa to stop, and promising they would be better; just so they didn't have to feel the pain anymore. Grandpa never hit Willa. She never knew why and never questioned it. Sometimes her brothers hated her for that and they would call her Grandpa's little pet rat. There were lots of times when they thought how unfair it was that they were the only ones to get beaten, and why not Willa, too?

Ron would question her, "What makes you any better than us?"

"I don't know," she explained to him, which was the truth. "It's not my fault. I never asked not to be hit," she said.

Willa thought about it, and if that was happening to her, she would feel the same way they did. She was glad she didn't get hit but it was not her idea. Maybe the reason behind it was because she prayed to God more than the boys did, and God kept her from the rage each and every time it happened. Grandpa didn't beat them every weekend, but it happened; that was enough to stop going over as often. Willa would pray to God, begging him to stop this. He did by keeping the boys home. They wouldn't go back to that house until they were older. Willa would also pray during these times asking God to please kill both Grandpa and especially Vesta for being so mean.

Since Willa is now the only one going to Grandpa's and Vesta's house on the weekend, she figured it was a way to keep the beatings from happening to her. It wasn't foolproof, but it usually worked every time she had to use it. The way she did it was that she would promise Vesta not to tell Grandpa when she was being mean and vicious to her. When Vesta would give Willa a bath and she would get soap in her eyes, and if Willa cried or said something about it to her, Vesta would rub the soap in deeper with her fist, turning it and making it even worse.

Then she would say to Willa, "Now you have something to cry about, you little brat."

Or there were the times when Vesta held Willa's head under water a little longer than necessary while she was rinsing the shampoo from her hair. When Willa tried to come up for air, Vesta wouldn't let her.

"You are old enough to do this yourself," Vesta would say. "If I had wanted to do this, I would have had a child with your grandpa."

Then there were the times when Willa was crying because she was being too rough. Vesta would grab her by the hair on the back of her head and start dunking her head into the water, bringing her up just long enough to gasp for a breath of air. Willa would get scared after it was all over. She cried and pleaded to Vesta to please stop. Vesta would then realize what she had done. Then she would promise not to tell Grandpa what bad children they were that day. So in return, she made Willa promise to keep her mouth shut, and so she did. When Willa did tell Grandpa, showing him her red eyes or other marks that Vesta had left on her, he would get so angry at her, and then he would beat Vesta. He would hit her in the face and on her body with his fist. He didn't care where they were; he hit her in front of the children. Sometimes Willa would feel sorry for Vesta, seeing her crying after Grandpa had hit her, or seeing her face swell up afterward. Willa would wish she hadn't said anything, but mostly there were the times when she told her grandpa because she thought Vesta deserved it. She often thought, "How could Vesta make up all the lies to get my brothers beaten so bad? She knew how brutal Grandpa could get, and she knew how hard he hit her. He wasn't any easier on the boys. She was always yelling at them about something—any little thing would set her off. She was always telling us what ungrateful and spoiled brats we were, and that we didn't appreciate anything. She accused us of taking her husband away from her on the weekends. These thoughts kept Willa strong enough to tell the next time Vesta was cruel to her.

Willa was so hurt within; she didn't know what to think most of the time. She hated Vesta, and not Grandpa. Willa was afraid of him. She was scared mostly of what he might do to her, even though he had never hit her. The fact still remains, he hit and hurt her brothers, and those were the two other people she loved so much besides Grandpa. No matter how much they fought with one another (sibling rivalry), they were still the closest to her heart, and they have been through so much together.

Willa thought, "I hate you, Vesta, and I wish one of the monsters in this house would take you away." These thoughts came from a seven-year-old little girl—a little girl who always tried to please everyone. She guessed she really didn't hate Vesta; she just hated the idea that no matter how hard they tried, Willa or her brothers could or would never please her. They would always get the blame for everything.

When the kids would try to tell Grandpa that Vesta was lying to cover up her drinking, he refused to listen to it. He believed Vesta and her stories about how they just didn't like her, and were making up some sort of vindictive lie to get her and him to fight. They started showing him where Vesta hid her bottles of whiskey, to prove their innocence, and to prove to him that they were not the ones lying. Vesta would keep finding new places to hide the bottles. However, being the nosy kids that they were, and also needing evidence, they would always find her new hiding places. They had to; it was survival for the boys, and their only protection. Let's not forget the times when Vesta tried to drown Willa in the bathtub. Willa questioned herself. "Is that so wrong to go digging up someone's personal things? Does that make me a bad girl? Does that make my brothers bad boys? I know we shouldn't be snooping around the house, but Vesta shouldn't be lying, either. She could go to hell and burn for eternity. Doesn't she care?"

When the kids got home and told their mom about what had happened, she wouldn't say a thing to either Grandpa or Vesta. The kids would tell her exactly what had happened—the reason why the boys came home with black eyes, swollen faces, and bruises all over their bodies. They told her, even though she never asked.

She would say, "I told you not to go over there. It is no fault but your own. You don't listen to me, so I don't want to hear about it."

"She doesn't care about us," we would whisper to each other when we went into another room. "She only cares about herself. She never tried to stop any of us from going over to Grandpa's house for the weekend," they whispered.

Willa sometimes felt as if nobody cared, that there were two innocent young boys being beaten by a grown man, with his fists, and they were getting kicked for no reason. They did nothing wrong. None of them did anything wrong. They were just victims of circumstance. Within her heart, and to God, Willa made a promise, that if she ever has any kids, she would treat them with dignity and respect. Willa and her brothers had no defense and she always felt so helpless. She never wants another human being to feel the way she does.

"If I have kids, I will always be there for them and protect them from any harm," she whispered.

CHAPTER EIGHT

At eight years old, there was yet another appearance. Willa was sitting in the living room, on the sofa that sat right along the wall where the long dark hallway was. She could see everything all the way into the kitchen. She was visiting alone—just she and Vesta had been in the house. It was early afternoon and Grandpa had left early to get a few errands done, Then, he was going to stop by one of the job sites before returning home. He let them know he wouldn't be home until supper time—around five o'clock. That left Vesta and Willa at the house alone, together. On this day, Willa didn't realize Vesta was in the kitchen drinking her whiskey. She didn't like when Vesta drank because she would get mean and start yelling at her for no reason. She thought Vesta was in there cooking, washing clothes, or doing one of the other many domestic chores she always complained about. She never complained about doing her "domestic duties" (that's how she referred to them) in front of Grandpa. Vesta also complained to Willa about Grandpa's cigar smoke.

"Why complain at me about it? I didn't tell him to smoke them. He was smoking those smelly things before I was born."

Besides, Vesta had no room to talk. She always had a Pall Mall in her mouth. There were ashtrays all over the house and there were plenty of tables to put them on. The house was always spotless but the smell of smoke was always in the air.

There were times when Willa felt very afraid during the day, because there was usually plenty of light shining through the long skinny windows. The daytime is usually quiet. When Grandpa was home, he would be sitting in his chair smoking a cigar and watching TV. Or, he would be at his desk smoking a cigar while he was working on his journals and ledgers. Vesta would be busy doing one of her many daily domestic chores. Willa would help Vesta sometimes by dusting the furniture and the woodwork around the floor, the doors, and the fireplace mantle. Then she would go to her mutual corner and color on one of the many coloring books that she had or she would play with her paper dolls. Vesta got the McCall's magazine and Willa cut out the Betsy McCall paper dolls from it. She kept them in a cigar box that Grandpa gave her. Willa also decoded the messages Betsy McCall would write each week. She never brought any toys from home because Vesta would complain that there was a mess, even if the toys were only around Willa on the couch.

On that day, Willa sat down to color in one of her new coloring books that Grandpa and Vesta had just bought. The house was quiet; the only noises she could hear were the ones Vesta was making in the kitchen. Everything is fine. This is a good day—a quiet day, a serene day, and maybe it was too quiet and peaceful. The sun was shining brightly through the windows. Willa wished she could go over and sit on the floor where the sun was shining in. She just wanted to feel the warmth that it was offering to her. The birds were chirping outside, and she could hear them so clearly. In the summertime, Vesta opens all the doors and windows to allow the fresh morning air into the house. It is such a beautiful summer day. Willa would have never thought in her wildest imagination that this day—as sunny, bright, and cheerful as it was—would bring gloom. She never suspected any bad could happen on that day.

Willa always sat with her back to the long dark hallway, ever since the day she and her brothers saw the devil standing in the dining room. She didn't trust anything, so she took that precaution. She heard a noise in the hallway; she knew it wasn't Vesta because she could hear the water running in the kitchen where she was preparing to make lunch for the two of them. She didn't look up or turn around. She figured it was probably just her imagination or maybe the mice were running around making noises. That wouldn't be unusual, because sometimes they heard noises while everyone was around.

Grandpa would say, "It's the house settling; it's so old it creaks."

So she ignored the noise and kept coloring, trying only to concentrate on the colors; closing her mind to her surroundings. About five seconds later, there it was again. She heard the same noise.

"I know I heard something this time," she said quietly.

This time it was much louder but it was the same. This time it aroused her curiosity. She figured if she would just turn her head a little and peek out of the corner of her eye, she could see nothing was there and then she could relax. She wanted to keep coloring. She started to feel the fear rising within her, and her heart started to beat a little faster. She turned her head and peeked, but to her surprise, nothing was there

"Thank God," she thought.

She didn't know what to expect or what she thought she would see. All she knew was that there was nothing there. There is absolutely nothing to worry about.

"Did I really want to see something?" she thought. This was strange because she really didn't know. "Nah, no way. Absolutely not. I don't think so."

By now, she was too afraid to move and too embarrassed to get up to go sit in the kitchen with Vesta. She would just tell her to go back into the living room and quit imagining things.

"I swear, that is the most paranoid troubled child on this earth."

These were the words Willa once heard Vesta telling Grandpa.

"She needs to learn how to use her imagination in a way that will prosper her in the future. But with the way she is going, she will most likely end up in some mental institution."

Willa was remembering those words.

"No, I can't go running to her. She will just get mad and have something else to complain about," she thought. She wondered if she sat quietly and tried to get back to her coloring, if everything would be all right. She wanted to prove to herself that her imagination and the mice were just playing tricks on her. Willa was coloring, putting her total attention to the details on the pictures, and making sure not to go outside of the lines. Then suddenly, there it is again; this time she heard it louder than the second time. It sounded like a loud thud, like someone falling on the floor. Her head snapped up and around, making her entire body face the kitchen.

Standing at the end of the long dark hallway was the most frightening looking witch she had ever seen (even in the movies). Willa could see every detail of the witch because her eyes had become fixed on her. She couldn't seem to close her eyes or look away from the witch. She was stunned. She was staring open-mouthed at it or her and the witch was staring back at her. Her face was green with black warts on it. There were worms crawling out of it, and blood was oozing out of the same places where the worms were coming out. Willa could see the worms wiggling, and looking like they were trying to get either in or out of the skin. It made her stomach start to turn. Then the witch started calling her name; just like the devil had known her name.

"Willa, come here, darling. Come to me, please. I have something really special to give you. Come see what it is," she cackled.

Willa's heart was beating so fast—pounding harder, faster and louder. The only thing she could think to do was to close her eyes and bury her head in the couch cushions and pillows, and then start screaming at the top of her lungs.

Shivering and shaking, too afraid to move, she could feel the witch's eyes staring at her. She could feel the heat burning into her flesh, and trying to reach for her soul.

"Leave me alone. Please don't kill me. I was being good. I didn't do anything wrong," she sobbed, hoping the witch would hear her and go away.

"I don't want to be here anymore," she thought.

Suddenly, she felt a hand reach down and touch her on the shoulder. She screamed louder, thinking, "She has me, and there is nothing I can do now." She felt her body going limp. Her head was spinning and everything went dark. The fear inside was more than she could handle. Then she heard Vesta's voice.

Thank God! The hand belongs to Vesta. She was relieved.

"What's wrong with you, child? Why are you screaming and burying your head?" she asked.

"There was an ugly witch at the end of the hallway. She was calling me, and telling me to come to her. She knew my name, Vesta," she said, crying hysterically. "I was being good today. I didn't do anything wrong. All I was doing was coloring. I wasn't making any noise. Was I bad today, Vesta?" she sobbed.

"First of all, no, you were not being bad today. You were very quiet, and I appreciate that. Second, there is no witch at the end of the hallway. Look and see. The only people in this house are you and me. There is no one else here. I can assure you that because as soon as I heard you screaming, I came running as fast as I could. Don't you think I would have bumped into her if she was there? Wouldn't you think so?"

Her words sounded so sincere and caring. Willa nodded her head, "Yes." All she could do was hold onto Vesta for now. Willa didn't want to let go of Vesta. She didn't want to leave her side for the rest of the day. She didn't mind the smell of the alcohol and cigarette smoke. She just didn't want to be alone anymore. Willa couldn't help to think back to something Vesta had said.

"As soon as I heard you screaming, I came running as fast as I could."

Willa felt as though she was alone and screaming for a long time. Does the time slow down when fear takes over? Why did she come and touch me on the shoulder? Did she call out to me and let me know she was there? Or did she just put her hand on me? Oh well, never mind. She is here now keeping me safe.

Willa felt that anytime Grandpa and even sometimes Vesta held her or when one of them was nearby, the evil beings would all stay away. Maybe the evil was scared of Grandpa and Vesta. Maybe Grandpa and Vesta were meaner than the demons, she thought. Maybe she saw these things because she wanted attention, just like Vesta and Esther said. "I don't know why I would want to scare myself so badly, just for the attention, she thought. Vesta tried to get up. She needed to get back to cooking lunch, but Willa wouldn't let her go.

She clung to her, pleading, "Please don't go. Don't leave me in here all by myself!" she begged

"I have to go. I have lunch on the stove cooking. I can't stay in here with you or the food will burn," she said. "You'll be okay. Lunch is almost finished."

Willa must have looked pretty pathetic, because Vesta, of all people, decided that it would be okay if Willa went into the kitchen with her while she cooked. One of the rules of the house is that everyone, including Grandpa, is to stay out of the kitchen while Vesta is in there cooking. As long as Willa promised to be quiet and sit still, it was okay, but for today only.

"I promise, you won't even know I am in there. I will be so good," she promised.

Willa grabbed her coloring book and crayons to take with her and she sat patiently coloring until lunch was finished. They both sat down to eat. Vesta made Willa's favorite food—grilled cheese sandwiches, French fries and vegetable soup. After lunch, Vesta informed her that she had to leave the kitchen.

"You have to go back to the front room," she said. "You can't stay in here because I need to clean up and decide what we are having for supper."

"But I want to stay in here with you. I can be very quiet. Please let me stay," she begged.

"You know the rules, Willa. You can go back to the living room or…" She stopped. "I know. How about going out back to play in the yard, or go out to sit on the front porch?" she suggested.

"Okay, I think I'll go out to sit on the front porch," she said.

Willa turned and left, dragging her feet, carrying her coloring books and crayons. It is boring to sit on the front porch, but it might be different now that Grandpa had new neighbors who moved into

Ruby's house. She didn't feel comfortable being out in the back yard by herself because she didn't know if it was her imagination or if she really saw it. She would sometimes see a face of a man looking out of the pantry window at her. Willa met the people who moved into the house, so she didn't know if the man who lived there was staring at her through the window or what. To tell you the truth, she doesn't even know if there is a man living in that house.

Grandpa returned home from his errands and all the other places he had to go to today. Vesta and Willa told him what had happened earlier today. He explained to her that the house had absolutely, "No demons, or witches," or anything of the sort.

"I have lived in this same house for many years, ever since your mother was a little girl the age of twelve. When we moved here, there were no demons then and there are none now. You are the only one who has seen any of these so-called demons and such. With the exception of the one time your brothers saw it with you," he said. "I don't understand you, Princess," he added.

None of them could understand why this was happening to her, or why she had such an over-active imagination. Grandpa took her on a tour of the house, especially around the dining room. He opened the couch into a bed to make sure there was nothing hiding underneath or inside it. Then he shook out the nicely folded blankets and sheets and even shook out the pillows.

"See? Nothing here," he said, showing her.

After that, they inspected the rest of the house, looking under the furniture, inside the drawers, and he even opened the doors to the closet that he made. Willa was afraid to look in there. She was afraid something might jump out and get both of them. Nothing was in there but a bunch of clothes that smelled of mothballs. Grandpa wanted to prove to her once and for all that there is nothing here in his house to be afraid of.

"You have a very over-active imagination; there is nothing to worry about," he told her.

"Oh, yeah," she thought. "I saw it. It was real and anyway I asked the nuns at school if there were such things and I was told that witches are known to have special powers enabling them to make themselves appear and disappear at random. They can also turn themselves into anything they choose. It could be something small like dust or something familiar to their prey. So there, Mr. Smart Pants," she thought. She really didn't want to stay at or go back to that house ever again, not ever. She didn't want to hurt anyone's feelings, so she kept going back time and time again.

CHAPTER NINE

There had not been an appearance for a long time. Things were going good on the weekends at Grandpa's house. Vesta was still drinking and complaining about one thing or another—not a really big change. The only difference was that now Willa had more control over her over-active imagination.

One evening when Willa was nine years old, she was feeling uncomfortable, as she had felt plenty of times before. All evening she kept feeling as though someone or something was staring at her, even though Grandpa and Vesta were there in the same room with her. It was weird and out of the ordinary. Willa usually felt more at ease with people around, especially Grandpa and Vesta, but not that night. It was an exception of her feeling unusually scared. She didn't say a word to anyone; she just kept to herself, knowing she would probably get into trouble for her paranoia. She was older now so that meant she had to do chores. One of the chores was to wash the dishes all alone after everyone had finished eating. That meant staying in the kitchen all alone while the mice played in the pantry behind her and to the left.

The mice made a lot of noise that sounded like someone was walking around in there. Sometimes Willa thought she heard breathing. Then there is the cellar door, which is to her left side while standing at the sink. The cellar door is scary just being there, with nothing happening to it. She knew it was there, and behind it, on the other side, there was total darkness. She wanted no part of that area of the kitchen because she wasn't 100 percent sure what was actually behind it.

The first thing Willa did before doing anything else was to make sure the table was firmly against the door. When the wind was blowing outside, it didn't make any difference because the door would hit against the table—opening closing, and pushing the table slightly away from the wall—little by little. When Willa first saw that happening, and even now sometimes, she thinks the monsters were behind the door trying to get out to grab her. When she first saw it happening, she got so scared that she ran into the living room where Grandpa and Vesta were watching TV.

She yelled, "There is someone in the cellar."

"What are you talking about?" Grandpa asked.

"The cellar door keeps trying to open but it can't because the table is in the way. It sounds and looks like someone is trying to get out of there," she said.

Grandpa and Vesta started laughing. Willa found nothing funny about it.

"Silly girl, when will it stop?" Vesta laughed. "That is the wind blowing through the window in the cellar," she added.

Wow, did she feel embarrassed and silly.

Willa was glad they always ate supper early every night especially in the winter, since it started getting dark outside earlier. If nothing else, there was still enough light outside coming in through the windows, to allow her to see everything in the surrounding area. Another rule of the house is no lights are to be on in any room that wasn't being occupied, and now she was tall enough to reach the string that had to be pulled to turn the lights on and off. She could no longer yell or go ask someone to come turn the light off for her anymore. Being smaller gave her that advantage and she missed those days. Each light had to be shut off as soon as whoever was in the room last left that room. Now that person is Willa, and the worst thing is that, she couldn't go to the room ahead of her, and turn that light on, and then go back and shut the one off behind her. Besides, the long dark hallway had no light to turn on or off. Since there was no one in the rooms between the kitchen and the living room after supper, all of the lights were shut off between them. The only light on should be the one in the room where everyone congregated to watch TV. Grandpa always watched Lawrence Welk. He made sure that everything would get done so he could watch that program. When it was a day that it wasn't on, there was always something else to watch. Vesta usually sat in her chair mending socks or was sewing on something. No matter how Willa felt about anything, it still didn't change the fact that she had to turn the lights off as soon as she left the kitchen or any other room she had to leave.

Most evenings she would go into the living room and sit down to relax when she felt the need to go to the restroom. It had already started to get dark and she was afraid to go back, so she sat acting like she was enjoying the evening, hoping the feeling would go away. Then when it was time to go to bed, all the lights were turned off—the usual ritual. Willa started feeling extremely uncomfortable and was now terrified to walk down the long dark hallway to go to the bathroom. She figured she would hold out until the morning. "I'm a big girl, no problem," she thought. Willa slept on the sofa bed in the front room, just beneath the picture of Grandma Emma. Her mother Esther told her the story of how Grandma Emma got cancer and she had to stay home to tend to her mother until she died—which was in Grandpa and Vesta's bedroom. Every time Willa looked at that picture, she would recall the story that her mom had told her. The family took pictures of Grandma Emma on her deathbed and showed them to the children. The pictures were taken from the time she got the disease up until she was lying in her coffin. The pictures were horrible; it was just plain sick watching her die, even if it was only in pictures. Willa had never met her Grandma Emma; she had died at the age of forty-four. Grandma Emma never got to see any of her four children get married. She died before she became a grandmother. Esther told Willa that Grandma Emma wanted to see her children walk down the aisle, get married, and have lots of children.

Willa crawled under the sheet and blanket, making sure her head was covered. She thought that if she was fully covered, especially her head, nothing could get her because they couldn't see her. Willa is so small and skinny there is hardly a lump in the bed. She said her bedtime prayers, like she did every night.

"Now I lay me down to sleep. I pray the Lord my soul to keep. If I soul die before I wake, I pray the Lord my soul to take."

Grandpa taught her that prayer a long time ago, when she began having the nightmares. He told her it was a shield to keep all evil away from her. Willa took that prayer seriously because the Lord is the only spirit whom she wanted to take her soul. She started tossing and turning because she needed to go pee. She was too big to wet the bed, but too afraid to go to the bathroom in the dark house. When she was younger, she could call out to someone and they would come get her and it was always Vesta, who would escort her to and from the bathroom. Willa would get into a lot of trouble if she tried that now. Grandpa and Vesta would question her on why she hadn't gone before going to bed. She could just hear them now. "What's wrong with you?

I thought you were over your childish paranoia. Get up and go to the bathroom. I don't want to hear another word from you." Vesta's words rang in her ears since she had heard them many times before. Willa said another little prayer.

"Please get rid of this feeling so I can get some sleep, and I promise I won't do this ever again. Next time, I promise to go while everyone is awake, while it is still light out."

How she wished she had gone while they were all still awake. That way, if there was anything or anyone in the bathroom trying to get her, she could scream and someone would come running to her rescue. Now they are sleeping and may not hear her screaming. By now, it is getting too hard to control the urge to pee because she is thinking about it too much. It is also cold in the house. Grandpa always turned the heat down at bedtime, saying the blankets will keep everyone warm throughout the night.

"Maybe if I close my eyes and feel my way to the bathroom, walking lightly and slowly, the demons and monsters won't hear me. It's worth the try. What could I lose? My Soul!"

Thoughts were reeling in her head.

She got up out of bed, keeping her eyes closed tightly. Her heart started beating fast, and butterflies were fluttering inside of her belly. She could feel the stares all around her. The hair on the back of her neck is standing up. "Will the prayer still work? I am no longer in bed. I am not asleep. The prayer says, 'Now I lay me down to sleep.'"

"God, please, let the prayer work, while I'm up and out of bed, please," she said quietly as she started walking toward the bathroom.

Feeling her way in the dark, and keeping her eyes closed, she felt the warm stares on her back and the heat from their eyes on her neck. Her heart is pounding so hard she is afraid someone or something will hear it echoing throughout the dark house. Maybe she might wake up

Grandpa or Vesta with the loud pounding within her. She didn't want to do that. She held her chest, trying to cover the sound. She kept inching her way forward, being as quiet as possible, and trying not to startle anyone or anything. She didn't want to make them mad enough to attack her. She didn't want them to rip her apart while she was still alive; she didn't want them to try to get her soul. Finally, she reached the hallway while keeping her eyes closed tightly. She kept feeling her way, and tried to be quiet. It seemed as though every floorboard had a creak in it no matter how lightly she walked. She finally reached the bathroom door; it's not over with yet. She thought, "I still have to get past the **CLOSET** door first." She ran in, feeling the string to pull. Finally the light went on. She looked all around making sure it was safe—nothing under the bathtub, under the sink, and the closet door was closed.

"Good, it's safe; I'm safe," she thought. Now that the room was scanned, it was safe to sit down and let go. "Ahh, now I can go to sleep," she thought. But now what do I do? I'm done. Oh God, I don't want to do this, but I have to. I have to go back down the hallway, this time with my back turned toward the dining room, the kitchen, and most of all, the pantry. She didn't know if something could get at her easier with her back turned. Maybe she could sleep in here in the bathtub. "No way, what if something grabs at me from underneath or what if whatever is in the closet comes out when the lights go out and gets me? I don't think so. I have to get back into bed. Not only could one of the things that were mentioned happen, but I know for sure Grandpa and Vesta would get mad at me for sleeping in the bathtub. Anyway, I have no blankets to keep me warm and it is freezing in here." Would I get into trouble if I left the light on? Yes, she knew the rules. She pulled the string, turning the light off, not caring about how much noise she was making. As she went running as fast as she could back to bed, her heart was beating fast, but she made it. She covered her head and was able to fall fast asleep.

The next morning, Vesta let her know she had heard her running through the hallway. She reminded her that she knew better than to do such a thing, especially late at night when everyone was sleeping or at least trying to get some sleep.

"You know that calls for punishment, don't you?" she asked.

"Yes, I'm sorry; it won't happen again. I was just cold and wanted to hurry up to get under the covers," Willa apologized.

"There is no excuse; you still have to be punished for it," Vesta warned.

Willa was punished but that was okay with her. She made it through the night. She was still alive and that was all she really cared about. The weekend is over anyway, and she can go home this afternoon after lunch. She is not going to have to worry about going through any anxieties for at least another week.

"Maybe, if God gives me the strength that I have been praying for, I will be able to tell them I don't want to come back to this house ever again. That way, I will never have to go through that again," she thought.

CHAPTER TEN

Here she is still nine years old; it is just weeks before her tenth birthday. Sometimes it seems like the years just creep by. Willa was sitting on the couch in the living room watching TV. It was another of those times when Grandpa was away running errands and taking care of whatever else needed taking care of. He informed Vesta he probably wouldn't be home until suppertime.

"I have lots of things I need to take care of today, so I probably won't get back home until supper," he told her.

Grandpa always left for work before Willa woke up in the morning. There were times when he was there when she woke up, but those were very rare times—normally only on Sunday. After they all came home from church, Grandpa would leave to do whatever he does. He always left Willa alone with Vesta, no matter how many times she tried to warn him how much Vesta hated her.

He said she was being paranoid.

"I know for a fact that Vesta happens to love you very much," he told her.

He told Willa that she had to make more of an effort to allow Vesta to show how much she cares about her.

Willa heard a noise that morning. It sounded like moaning, as if someone was in pain. She called out to Vesta, wanting to make sure it was her, and hoping she was just drunk and making noises. Willa wanted to be sure that it was not someone or something else. There was no response to her summons, which sent a chill up her spine. She started to get flashbacks to that last day she spent over at Ruby's house. It is much earlier in the day than that day. It is around three o'clock in the afternoon. She got up to start her walk down the hallway to go to the kitchen. She was calling out for Vesta and was walking very slowly. She was walking with her left shoulder leaning against the wall and keeping herself as far away from the two doors as she possibly could. No matter how hard she tried to keep her eyes focused straight ahead of her, she couldn't. For whatever strange reason, she couldn't keep her eyes off the bathroom door.

"I don't want to do this," she thought. "I really should go back and call Vesta from the living room."

She stopped between the bedroom door and the bathroom door; she couldn't go any further. Her legs wouldn't let her move any further down the hallway. The hair all over her body was standing on end by now.

"I don't want to see her if she is dead," she thought. "I can't just turn my back on her. She may need me."

Thoughts were reeling in her head. "If she is dead, what should I do?" She got the courage to start walking toward the kitchen again, only taking a couple of steps, when all of a sudden he jumped into the hallway from the bathroom, stopping her dead in her tracks. There he stood, big (looking about ten feet tall, maybe even taller), red (almost as if he was dripping with someone's blood), maybe Vesta's blood! Willa didn't know if it was her imagination or if he really was drooling blood that was dripping on the floor. He is ugly! She could see the veins poking out from his neck, forehead and temples, and he was mean looking. It's the devil himself, reaching out to her, moving slowly toward her.

"Willa, my child, come to me. I've got you now. There is no getting away this time. You are mine and I have come to take you home with me."

Those were the words she heard him saying. She was too much in shock and in fear to turn around and run; or even to scream.

Willa thought her heart was going to jump out of her throat. She felt as though it was right there ready to come out, and it was just stuck there. Her head started spinning at that point. The only things she was able to hear were her heart pounding and her own thoughts. Her legs gave way.

"Why can't I scream, and save myself?" she thought. "If I could scream, Vesta might be able to hear me and she can come to save me. That is, if the devil hasn't gotten to her. Maybe that is her blood he is drooling. OH GOD! That means I am all alone. I'm not strong enough to fight him. He has me where he wants me."

Her wildest dreams and fears are coming true right now.

"Please let this be a dream. If it's a dream, it won't really be happening and I could wake up safe in bed. But I don't remember falling asleep, so it has to be real. It is not a dream. I'm all alone, just him and me. There is nobody else. They are all gone. I am going to die." These thoughts were spinning in her head as she was sobbing.

Willa felt herself falling, being sucked into what seemed to be a big black hole of a long dark tunnel. All the while, she kept falling and spinning.

"God, if you can hear me, please take me now. Please let it be you to get my soul. Don't let him get it. It belongs to you."

It was now getting harder for her to breathe; she could feel herself gasping for air. Her head was spinning. It also felt as though her body was in a spin. Her entire being was spinning around and around, and then everything went dark.

Willa could hear Grandpa and Vesta calling to her, and telling her to wake up. At first, their voices seemed unreachable, and so far away. She couldn't see either of them and could only see the darkness of wherever she was. As she started to ascend from the tunnel or hole, she could hear their voices a lot better and clearer. The next thing that happened (this was about a half hour later, from the time she had heard the noise), she woke up lying on the couch. She didn't remember anything between the time she passed out until the time she woke up. If she had to tell the story of what happened in that period of time, she would not be able to answer.

"You're going to be okay. We are here with you. What happened?" Grandpa asked, with a concerned look on his face.

Her head was still spinning and she felt sick to her stomach. She told them what happened—the story she remembered.

"This story is getting old, but it is true. This is real to her," Vesta said. "I heard you screaming. I called out to you, and when you didn't respond, I came running to find out what was wrong. That is when I found you lying in the hallway on the floor."

Willa didn't understand how she could hear her screaming, because she remembers how she tried to scream but couldn't.

Vesta went on saying, "When I saw you lying on the floor, breathing heavy, and repeating the prayer, 'Now I lay me down to sleep, I pray the Lord my soul to keep, If I should die before I wake, I pray the Lord my soul to take,' that's when I ran to call your Grandpa. You had us worried, Willa."

"What is going on in your life that you would have such a horrible experience? Is there something you're keeping in? Are you afraid of telling us or anyone else about a bad experience? And now you are facing your personal demon this way?" Grandpa asked.

"No, I don't think so," she said.

To herself, she thought, "The only thing I am keeping in is the fact that I'm afraid of this house and I never want to come back again." She wouldn't admit to that, no way—that would only hurt his feelings.

Willa never told her mom about the scary things that were happening to her at Grandpa's house, because she knew that if he (Grandpa) didn't believe her, her mom would definitely not believe her. Besides, no one did anything for her brothers, and Esther didn't care about anyone but herself. That is why she kept it all in—it was her own secret. She liked going over to Grandpa's anyway because she could pretend to be an only child. It is not as if it happened every time she went to visit. It only happened every once in a long while. She never knew when it was going to happen, and that reason itself was the scariest part—the anticipation of things to come. At least her bad dreams stopped. She hadn't had one in a long time. Maybe these appearances are all dreams. "Is my life a dream? Am I real?" she thought.

Chapter Eleven

One weekend, not the same as the others, she was feeling a little more comfortable, and more confident than she usually did. It seemed to be brighter in the house that night, and in the summer, it was normally brighter. Everyone went to bed and like she had done before, she didn't go to the bathroom before going to bed. However, this time she didn't feel the need for it—not until she got comfortable in bed. She covered up her head and said her prayers. She then tried to go to sleep. It didn't work like it hadn't worked the times before this. She got up, this time with her eyes open. She felt more confident, plus the fact that she was now ten-and-one-half years old. She felt she should no longer be afraid. She hadn't had any bad dreams or any confrontations in a long time, since just before she turned ten years old. She was finally able to control her paranoia. Everyone was proud of her and she was proud of herself.

The first thing she saw when she got out of bed was the picture of Grandma Emma hanging on the wall over the sofa where she slept. She started to remember the story her mom had told her about Grandma

Emma. It sent a chill up her spine. The picture seemed to be staring at her and watching her every move. She found it hard not to stare back at the picture. Usually when she would get afraid of something, she would stare at it, whether she wanted to or not. She turned around and there's the elk head above the fireplace—"Grandpa's pride, his trophy," staring down at her, both of them following her with their eyes, and both of them dead. One is only a picture and the other is a stuffed trophy. She was getting stared at front and back, right side and left— no matter which way she turned. In a way, she somehow found it sort of fascinating but she also thought that somehow each of them were aware. They know something and they are alive somehow, yet they are both dead. She started to get scared. She could feel the fear rising within her. The hair on the back of her neck felt as if someone were running their fingers through it. She was deep in thought, wondering why they were staring at her. "Am I going to be okay?" She shivered at the thought, and then snapped out of it. "What's the matter with me? This isn't supposed to be happening to me. I wasn't feeling scared when I went to bed tonight. I'm older now; I am able to control my fears and my imagination. Nothing is going to happen to me," she thought. She decided to close her eyes just to be sure and to be on the safe side. She figured she may as well. She would feel more secure that way. Besides, it was extremely dark on the way to the bathroom, and it would feel as though she had her eyes closed anyway. When it's that dark and her eyes are open, they usually got irritated anyway because she couldn't see a thing. She would be straining them by trying too hard to see where she was going.

She started walking slowly and quietly toward the bathroom. She could feel the coldness of the stares behind her. "Quit thinking like that," she reminded herself. When she reached the hallway, it suddenly felt warmer, (eerier) like someone or something was directly in front of her. She wanted to open her eyes, turn around, and just make a run for it back to bed. She wanted to forget all about going to the bathroom. It's warm in the house anyway. She probably wouldn't be tossing and turning, keeping herself awake because it was too cold. The summer nights didn't make the house cold. "Maybe I can go to sleep and not think about it until the morning? Nah! I've come this far. I may as well go all the way. Nothing is going to hurt me—nothing," she thought. She felt the need to open her eyes to see, just in case she needed to turn and run from whatever was staring at her. That way, it couldn't get her and she could have saved herself from some terrible confrontation. "Quit with the paranoia, Willa," she thought. "Stop with the stupidity already." She didn't open her eyes. She kept them closed and she figured it was just her active imagination again because of Grandma Emma's picture, and the elk head hanging above the fireplace.

She kept feeling her way in the dark. She got closer to the wall on the left side making sure her left shoulder was rubbing against it. Due to her paranoia, she decided to extend her right hand in front of her, and she swayed it back and forth. She wanted to be able to feel for anyone or anything that may be in her way. "What if I step on a mouse or a rat that happens to be running through the hallway? Yuck, what a sick mind you have," she thought. "That could happen and if the rodent gets scared it could bite me and give me a disease or something. Ick, get that thought out of your mind." She could almost feel the furry little body under her feet, which gave her the creeps and made her shiver at the thought. She progressed slowly down the hallway with her eyes shut, and paid attention to her feet as well as everything else. Suddenly, out of nowhere, she felt a body. She could feel the blood rush through her body, sending bolts of lightning through her veins. Her heart stopped for just a second or two. She opened her eyes slowly; she was desperately hoping it was the wall on the other side, even though it felt soft and lumpy like a body. She still had her hopes that it could be a wall.

Standing in front of her was a person. That's just how her luck is; it couldn't be the wall. It was too dark to see anything clearly. There was absolutely no way her eyes could focus now, especially since she was terrified. She couldn't tell who or what it was or if it was a he or a she. All she could see was a big round dark shadow of someone. It could be anybody, but, "Could it possibly be...?" She didn't want to think of who it could be. Whoever it was didn't talk. It didn't say anything. Again, she couldn't scream or run. All she could do was drop from where she was standing. Her head started spinning around and her heart was racing at top speed. It was beating so fast that she thought it would come right out of her body. She felt as if she were going to throw up right then and there. She laid there in the fetal position thinking about the past year. She had come so far with her fears and now she was curled up on the hallway floor waiting to be devoured by whatever was standing above her. She felt an ice-cold hand touch her. She thought she was going to die. "I'm caught; it's over," was the only thought that she had.

She heard Vesta's voice. It was not an evil demon. Then again, Vesta/demon—which is scarier? Vesta just so happened to be coming out of the bathroom on her way back to her bedroom when Willa was on her way to the bathroom. Vesta walked Willa to the bathroom and turned on the light for her, because she was still a little weak from the scare she just had.

"Vesta, why didn't you say anything out there in the hallway?" Willa asked.

"Because, I thought you knew who I was. I didn't realize you had your eyes closed," she explained.

"But, you didn't say a word. That's what scared me even more," Willa explained. "I didn't know what or who to expect to be standing in front of me," she added.

"Didn't you hear the toilet flush?" Vesta asked.

"No," she said.

"Well maybe next time you come to the bathroom in the dark, you will keep your eyes open so you can see, huh," she added.

"Yea, I guess so, but will you stay in here with me until I'm done?" Willa asked.

"Sure, but you better hurry because I'm exhausted and I have to get up early."

Vesta stayed with Willa until she was done; she turned the light off and walked her as far as her bedroom.

When Willa got to bed, she lay down, covered her head and tried to go to sleep, but she couldn't. She kept thinking about the incident in the hallway. "Did Vesta do that on purpose? Did she really think that I knew who she was? Maybe she heard me get out of bed and she hurried into the hallway to scare me? I know that I would have heard the toilet flush because it is loud." She tried to blank her mind from the thoughts but it was hard. It didn't seem like an accident. It seemed now that it was set up to be that way to scare her for some reason. She knew all along that Vesta could be cruel, but to do such a thing in the night to someone she knows has a problem with the unknown and sudden happenings, is the cruelest thing she could do to her. Willa wondered if Vesta hated her so much and that was the reason she stood in the dark—just to scare her. Willa couldn't tell Grandpa because what if Vesta was telling the truth and it was a coincidence. She would be getting Vesta into trouble for nothing, just because of her paranoia. "If it was just a cruel joke that she played on me, God will punish her," she thought.

She tossed and turned, thinking of ways she could find out if Vesta was telling the truth or not. If she wasn't, Willa could plan an attack of retaliation. "I could show Grandpa where her new stash of whiskey is because I ran across it accidentally today when she had me cleaning the bathroom. Maybe I could tell him about the cruel joke she pulled on me." Thoughts were reeling through her head. Willa dreamed that night about Vesta being a big ugly witch and she would try to get her, chasing her through the house while Grandpa was away. Vesta caught her, and was torturing her. She pulled her hair out of her head and made bald spots all over her head. Vesta told Willa that Grandpa was out doing errands, but she really killed him and put him in the cellar for the rats to eat at his body. Willa woke up a couple of times that night and tried to dream something more pleasant, but the dream somehow kept going back to the same bad nightmare.

Chapter Twelve

Willa started having the nightmares again, the ones about the man in the pantry. He was calling her and threatening her with the mice, while either her head was huge and her body too small, or her body extremely large with her head being too small. The eerie part about it all was that she could actually feel parts of her body growing and stretching. There was also a stench each time it was happening. It was the smell of wet dirt—not the fresh smell of dirt after it rains—but more stale. It's kind of hard to describe. Willa woke up in the middle of the dream a couple of times sweating and panting, and trying to catch her breath. She found it hard to swallow. Her throat was so dry that when she did swallow, the inside of her throat would stick together. She didn't want to get out of bed to go into the pantry to get a glass for some water. When she was home, she didn't want to get up to go downstairs to get a drink of water. She was frightened. The dream seemed so real. Maybe the man made her throat dry that way so he could lure her into the pantry to get her. She tried going back to sleep knowing she would dream again. This way she would be able to wake herself up. Most times, it would work, but there were the few when she had to wake herself up screaming, because he was right in front of her, ready to grab her and take her soul.

It was Friday again, and she knew Grandpa would be over to get her. "Is there a good excuse I could give for not wanting to go over this weekend?" she thought. "I'm not feeling sick and even if I were sick, he would take me over to his house. Then he would take me to a doctor to get checked. I can't win. There is no excuse," she thought. Home wasn't any better. She was having the nightmares at both houses. At Grandpa's, she would have the peace and quiet during the day. She needed someone to talk to, but her brothers had their own lives and other interests. Those were better than listening to her. She couldn't talk to her mom because she was always busy.

Esther once told her, "I don't know what to tell you, Willa. Maybe you are possessed by the devil—could be Satan himself."

That made Willa more afraid than she had already been. If she stayed at home, she would be in trouble for some reason or another. She would get accused of doing some kind of ungodly thing with her brothers or with her stepfather, Jacob. She didn't know why her mom accused her of doing those things, but her thoughts on it were that her mom had a warped sense of humor. Esther would laugh after she had said some of the ugly accusations, like it was meant to be funny. It was anything but funny. It always made Willa feel so dirty for a long time whenever Esther made any of the accusations.

Willa was afraid to be alone with either of her brothers or with Jacob for fear of being accused of being a whore who lures the guys to do the unspeakable to them. She was the one accused most of the time. The poor boys and Jacob were Willa's victims, and they were powerless over her lustful ways. It makes her ill just to think of doing any of the things Esther said she was doing. Sometimes Willa's mind wondered if

Ester and her brothers, and maybe even Grandpa, did any of the things she was accused of doing. "It could be Esther's own guilt she is accusing me of. Maybe she was the luring whore," she thought. While at home, Willa mostly stayed in her bedroom behind a locked door. There were a few times when she was accused because the door was locked.

"Did you have someone climb in the window?" Esther would ask accusingly.

"No, I was in here all by myself," she retaliated.

"I heard you talking to someone in here. It sounded like a man's voice. Who was it?" she accused.

"There was no one in here with me. You probably heard the man on the radio," she cried.

"Go ahead and cry. Your tears are not going to work on me. I know guilt when I see it," Esther accused. "Sure, I believe you," she said, adding her sarcasm.

Then she turned around and left the room, giving Willa a look of disbelief. Willa just wanted to be alone in her room all by herself. Is that too much to ask? Now she feels so dirty because she is accused again. Willa's thoughts on a daily basis were, "I can't win! Why do I even try?" There were times—although few—when Esther would go to the store and Willa would be in her room crying because of something Esther had said. Jacob would come in and try to comfort her.

"Whether it makes any difference or not, I want to let you know that I believe in you. I know you are a good girl. Right now, your mom can't see that, but just know that there is someone besides you who knows. You are not alone. I get accused also. If anyone heard how your mom accuses me, I would get put into prison for child molestation. I'm just as scared as you are, and there are times I want to sit in a corner and think about the things that are going on around me. Don't worry, it will get better," he explained.

It got to the point where Willa was afraid to take a bath. Sometimes she was accused of taking one to get the smell of sex off her body. Willa can remember the first time she was accused of it—the memory is so clear. On that day, it was about four o'clock in the afternoon.

"Does anybody need to go to the bathroom before I go in to take my bath?" she asked everyone.

They all said no, except for Esther. She said she needed to go. She went into the bathroom, and then when she came out, she went into Willa's bedroom.

"Why are you going in to take a bath so early in the day?" she questioned.

"Because I'm feeling cold and I want to get the chill out of my bones," Willa explained.

"Yea, I saw Jacob up here while you were in your room. Don't think for one minute that I am stupid, Willa. I know what is going on. You need to get the smell of sex off of your body—that way you think I won't be able to smell it. Too late. I can smell it. I smelled you when you went downstairs. Don't try to hide anything from me, you whore. I don't like to be made a fool of," she roared.

Then Esther slapped Willa as hard as she could, which made her black out for just a second or two. Willa tried to hold back the tears.

"Don't cry, don't let her see you cry, don't give her the satisfaction of seeing the hurt she has caused you," Willa thought. It was much too impossible. She could feel the warmth of her tears rolling down her cheeks no matter how hard she tried to hold them in. The reason why she started crying wasn't only because Esther slapped her so hard, but because she was being accused of having sex and nothing happened. She didn't do anything. "I'm not a bad person; at least I try not to be," she thought. This is mostly the reason why Willa never refused to go over to Grandpa's house on Friday evenings. Hurt feelings are the main reason, but she couldn't handle being at home all day long. "What would I be doing to the guys then?" she thought. She wanted to get away from the abuse at home, which wasn't any better than the abuse she got at Grandpa's. Because of the hurt and anger, it would sometimes take Willa a week and sometimes even longer to stop the tears, and to get over the hurt.

Willa couldn't win. Most of the time she cried. She would go into her bedroom closet to cry alone so she wouldn't be heard. She tried to prove to Esther what a good girl she really was. "I love her. I only wish that sometime, anytime she would return the feeling." She cried, remembering. Whenever Willa told Esther, "I love you," Esther would just nod her head and walk away. Willa felt sorry for herself because she saw in her friends and their mother's relationships the love they have for each other. "Why can't my mom love me?" she sobbed. Willa felt that she was the true Cinderella that someone came into her life and wrote a story about. "I am always wrong; I am a whore; I am the slave," she thought as her tears increased. "Maybe mom is really my evil stepmother and she probably killed my rich father because he caught her treating me bad and she didn't like him defending me, so he had to die," she thought. The story told to her about her dad was that he was still alive, and he left Esther when she was pregnant with Serge. None of Esther's family has seen or heard from him since. "Hmm, I wonder, did she kill him? What did she do with his body?" she thought. Willa often wondered about her dad. She wondered if he was thinking about her; if he knew what was happening to her, and would he come and take her away from it all so she could live a happy life. It doesn't hurt to dream, does it? "It could be possible. It could happen even to me," she hoped. Willa spent a lot of time in her closet dreaming, crying, and being quiet about it all. She made sure Esther didn't see her cry. Esther's interpretation of Willa's tears meant Willa was guilty of doing or wanting to do something sick and ungodly. Willa often wondered why Esther didn't give her up for adoption since she irritated her so much and gave her so much grief. "Was it so she could have someone to torment? Was I just an easy target? I have heard you tell Jacob and Serge, 'I love you.' Why not me? Why not Ron?" she thought. "What wrong did we ever do to you? We have only bent over backwards to try to please you." Her thoughts continued. "Don't cry, please don't cry, if you do and she sees the tears, she will accuse you of doing or thinking something wrong." She told herself this on the days she was feeling sorry for herself while trying to hold back the tears. Willa got good at holding back her tears in front of people, but there were times when it was just too much to ask of herself. She would often curl up in a sitting position with her head on her knees in a corner of the closet and sob until she fell asleep.

"I'm going to be brave this weekend." She often thought, "I am too old to be afraid of things conjured up in my imagination. Besides, what's worse—the monsters that don't exist anywhere else but in my imagination, or the real life demons I have to face on a daily basis? I will have to choose imagination. I guess if I tried hard enough, I could get rid of them. However, the ones I have to face in real life I'm stuck with until I am old enough to move out and live on my own. Maybe I'll escape when my 'Prince Charming' comes along and takes me away from it all." Thoughts raced in her mind. Willa never told Grandpa or Vesta about the accusations at home because she thought they would believe anything Esther told them. "I'm innocent but I alone believe in me and so does God—he does too," she thought. "God knows what I do and what I see. He is all I need besides myself." There were so many times Willa wished she could tell Grandpa or even Vesta what was going on, but she was alone with her dilemma—alone to see and feel her own fears and tears. Willa couldn't even tell her best friends at school because she was afraid they would choose to believe Esther since she was older and supposed to know what she was talking about. Maybe they wouldn't want to be her friend anymore because if they did believe her mom, they would probably think Willa was the whore she had been accused of being. Not to mention her imagination and dreams—they are pretty morbid most of the time—even to her and she is the one having them. Willa didn't want to lose her friends because they were all she had left of her sanity. With them, she could be the little girl that she really was.

Grandpa made his work schedule so he could spend more time on the weekend with Vesta and Willa.

He said, "So we can spend more time getting to know one another. It also gives us a chance to go places together."

Grandpa meant well, he really did. He set his schedule to where he would work every other Saturday each month and this Saturday was the one he had to work.

"I'll be gone for about five hours today. I am not staying all day today," he explained.

Vesta was supposedly feeling sick that weekend. She didn't like the idea that he brought Willa over to the house anyway, knowing he had to work.

"I'm sick and what is she going to do all alone? Is she going to scream all day because she is seeing monsters?" she questioned.

"I told you, Vesta, I will only be gone for about four or five hours at the most," Grandpa explained to her, sounding irritated and angry.

"Is he blind? Can't he see that she's just drunk, like the numerous times before? Can't he see that she hates me?" she thought. Willa wished she could disappear and go somewhere—a place where she would be welcome—somewhere, where she would be appreciated for herself. She wanted to be welcomed with open arms, even knowing that she has nightmares and is afraid of the dark. She wanted someone to accept her for who she is, if only there was such a place.

"Is he blind to the fact that she hates me and doesn't want anything to do with me? She will verbally torture me for this, I know she will," she thought. Willa tried to make an attempt to go back home.

"Maybe, I shouldn't stay this weekend if Vesta is sick. I might catch whatever it is she has and I don't want to miss any school this year, since it is my first year in public school. I don't want to ruin that. I can't be missing any days, and besides I don't know how the public school system works yet."

She rambled, not giving him a chance to get a word in.

"Vesta would probably be more comfortable if she were left alone. I have plenty of things I could be doing at home," she finished.

"Nonsense, Vesta probably needs you more now, to help her with the housework and other chores. Don't worry. Whatever is ailing her, I am sure it is not contagious."

He left it at that. Willa tried her best to get out of Vesta's hair. She gave it her best and Vesta was right there to witness it. Willa was hoping that Vesta would appreciate the effort she made.

"Did you hear that, Vesta? I'm trying and it's not working," Willa thought. "Why can't I disappear? I'm not wanted. I'm all alone. I have no one but myself. I don't want to do this anymore," she thought. Somehow and in some way, that weekend went well. Willa stayed outside in the back yard after she vacuumed and dusted. She stayed out of Vesta's way so there would be no problem.

CHAPTER THIRTEEN

As soon as Willa and her brothers were old enough, Esther enrolled them into St. Francis Catholic school. Esther then took them out of Catholic school when Willa was eleven years old, because Willa was doing things she shouldn't have been doing. A couple of the nuns at that school were teaching Willa and a few other girls how to conjure up bad spirits, and to make potions and spells to use against others. Esther never would have found out if Willa hadn't asked if she and her friends could use the outside storage room, since it wasn't being used for anything anyway. Willa and her friends thought it would be really cool to have their very own clubhouse, and to do the things they were doing with the nuns in the basement of the church.

A couple of nuns called Willa into the school's office after school one day.

They told her, "God came to us last night. He told us that you are one of the chosen few. We would like you to stay after school on Tuesday and Thursday afternoons each week. How would you feel about that?" they asked.

"Okay, but I'll have to tell my mom so she won't worry about where I am," Willa explained.

"Don't worry about that. We already called her to let her know that you will be staying and she gave us her permission to keep you over on those afternoons," they informed her.

Willa thought she was the only one who was going to be staying late, but to her surprise, there were other girls there as well. They didn't meet in a classroom; they all met in an abandoned bathroom down in the basement of the church. At first, Willa was scared. She wondered why they were going down to the dark basement. The first meeting they had was to let them know the reason they were chosen, and why they were all there. They let the girls know the rules of their meetings.

"This is sort of a secret club; absolutely no one can know what we do in this club. You cannot tell anyone, even your parents, what we do or say in this club. Do you all understand?" Sister Mary Helen asked.

"Yes, but what if our parents ask what it is we do. What are we supposed to tell them?" a girl named Elizabeth asked.

"You can tell them that you are learning the way that God meant for you, which will be the truth," Sister Mary Helen explained.

"But, what if they want us to tell them details? What if they ask what ways are those that you are talking about? What do we tell them then?" Elizabeth asked curiously.

"You will find a way not to tell them. As we get into the teachings, you will better understand the reason why you cannot tell anybody," Sister Mary Helen explained to everyone.

In the beginning, Willa was intimidated by it all, First, she was meeting new people and she was never good at meeting people. It was always somewhat hard for her. She couldn't seem to look at them until she got to know them. Second, she was scared because she didn't understand 'why the secrecy?' What's the big deal? That first meeting was creepy to Willa but that first meeting was nothing compared to the meetings that followed. It was after the weekend, and everyone had gone back to school on Monday. After the last class, Sister Mary Claire, even though it was hard to see her face because of the habit—she was a very beautiful woman and was probably in her twenties. She was standing outside of Willa's classroom when she got out of class.

"Remember, tomorrow we all will meet at the same place."

"Okay, I'll remember," Willa replied as she was putting on her coat to run out of the school so she could hurry into the church to pray before going home.

The next day when Willa walked downstairs to the basement, she felt a little scared because she wasn't completely sure she should be there. She went into the bathroom to see that this really was the meeting place. Not everyone had arrived when she walked in.

"Hi, Willa! I am glad to see you showed up," Sister Mary Helen greeted her with a big smile on her face.

Sister Mary Helen looks young like she's in her early thirties but she is somewhat on the round side. Everybody was greeted in a cheerful manner as they entered. The girls were all told to sit Indian style with legs crossed on the floor, in a circle, and facing each other. Sister Mary Claire was the last one to arrive.

"Girls, today we are going to learn chants. Do any of you know what chants are?" she asked.

Willa raised her hand, and she was gestured to go ahead and speak.

"A chant is a group of words, that are repeated," she explained.

"Yes, that's basically what a chant is. We are going to learn how to chant in a different language. It's an ancient Egyptian language. What these chants will do is summon up good spirits. What I mean by spirits is that we all have a soul. We call them a spirit, and when we die, the spirit of all living creatures lives on in what we know as 'the spirit world.' Sister Mary Helen will teach you all the first chant. You will need to pay close attention because there will be no paperwork for you to learn from. So remember, it is very important to give us your complete and undivided attention. You will have to memorize all of your teaching here in this room, because don't forget, this is a secret club," she explained to the girls.

"The first words I am going to teach you are very important. After I say each word, you must repeat it at least five times or more until we learn a complete sentence," she said.

They all started repeating the words. Each day when they met, they had about five words to remember. They had to make sure not to forget the words. So, they chanted the words they had learned previously before learning the new ones.

Willa thought about how the words they all chanted had sounded scary, even though she had no idea what they meant and how they said them with the group. As time progressed, it brought to mind a movie she had once watched that was scary. The people were chanting the words which sounded like the ones she was now chanting. In the movie, the people were doing this to conjure up the dead—bringing them to life. Willa didn't know if she wanted to stay or leave because it was now getting scarier every time she learned more words. "Do I want to learn the way that is meant for me?" she thought. "I guess I have to give it a try." Willa didn't feel comfortable with any of the things they were doing in the group, but as time went on, it got a little easier. She started to feel a lot better and it no longer bothered her. All of the girls in the secret club became very close to one another. They ate lunch together and hung out in their own special little group, away from everybody else. Even when they were not in school, the girls had their exclusive group and no one else was invited. They spent all their time with each other, except on the weekends when Willa was away visiting Grandpa and Vesta. The girls were told they had a so-called 'Gift from God,' and none of them knew what those words meant and no one ever questioned them. Willa just knew that when she was with the group, she felt special, wanted and needed.

After six months, the girls started to learn how to use the words appropriately to conjure up the spirits of the dead through a form of séance and meditation, using the chants that were taught to them before. The most scary spirit that they called was the spirit of Lady Catherine. They had no idea who or what any of these spirits were, but Lady Catherine was the spirit who came most of the time. When the group was meditating, their eyes had to stay closed at all times, thus keeping the bad spirits from entering into their bodies. A box of crayons was kept above the sink that was directly below a large mirror.

When the group first met Lady Catherine, Sister Mary Helen asked, "Who are you? We need to know who we are talking to," she told the spirit.

"Open your eyes," the spirit demanded. "Look to the mirror."

Lady Catherine talked through Sister Mary Claire most of the time, but there were times when she wrote messages on the mirror. The first time they met Lady Catherine she wrote her name on the bathroom mirror with a red crayon that looked as if it had been melted after she used it. They all knew that they had to keep their eyes closed, but ever so slightly, they squinted to see what was going on. There was the writing of her name and an image of a beautiful young woman inside the mirror that disappeared quickly. Fear filled up the room and the girls jumped up from where they were sitting. They ran upstairs and out of the church. They all were thinking about never going back into that bathroom again. The event that took place in the bathroom that day was something none of them ever expected. It was too real. Both of the sisters came outside.

"Come back in here. You all can catch a cold; it's too cold to be standing out here without a jacket," Sister Mary Helen demanded.

"We don't want to go back. What if the ghost comes back?" Elizabeth said, shivering.

"Don't worry, she's gone. We all saw that she left," Sister Mary Helen explained.

Everyone went inside the school, and called their mothers to come pick them up.

"Don't let what happened in the basement scare you. It shows that whoever saw it, truly has the gift of insight," she told them. "Remember, nothing can hurt you when you walk with God. I will see you on Thursday, right?" she said.

They all nodded their heads and then left.

The biggest moment came in December; they were all instructed by Lady Catherine to chant. They were handed a piece of string. Each of them had to hold the string while chanting, and then they were instructed to tie a knot in the middle of the string.

"Open your eyes, and look to the mirror," Lady Catherine through Sister Mary Claire instructed them. "There is a name printed next to your name. You must drop the piece of string you were handed on the front porch or the doorstep of the family whose name is printed next to your name," they were instructed.

The name that appeared next to Willa's, said "Allens."

"Does she mean the Allen family who live next door to me?" Willa asked.

"Yes, that is the first family who needs to be saved in your neighborhood," Sister Mary Helen informed her.

"I know them. My mom and Mrs. Allen are best friends," Willa explained.

Sister Mary Helen said, "Since this is a secret mission of God's, we don't want anybody to suspect anything. Therefore, it is Christmastime, you will go over to their house and try to sell them some Christmas candies. That will give you the opportunity to drop the string while no one is looking. Does everyone understand? No one must see you drop the string," she said, making it very clear.

Everyone nodded their heads in agreement. The girls all got their boxes of candy and then they left for home. Willa went to the Allen's house that evening. She knocked on the door, and Mrs. Allen answered.

"Hi, Mrs. Allen, I am selling these Christmas candies for my school. Would you like to buy some?" Willa asked politely.

"How much are you selling them for?" she asked.

"Fifty cents a box," Willa explained.

"Sure, I'll take two boxes. Would you like to come in and wait while I go get the money?" Mrs. Allen asked.

"No, thank you, I will wait here," Willa, said.

Mrs. Allen turned to go get the money, which gave Willa the opportunity to drop the string on the porch.

"Thank you," Willa said as she left, proud of herself at what she had just done.

"They are going to have a Merry Christmas," she thought. "God is going to save their souls."

When Willa got home from school the next day, Esther was sitting on the couch crying.

"What's wrong?" she asked.

"You are too young to understand," Esther said.

"I want to try to understand. Maybe I can help you," Willa said, trying to comfort her mom.

"YOU HELP? HAH, this will be interesting! Let us see what you can do. Listen to this, the entire Allen family passed away last night from poisonous gasses. The entire family is dead, all of them. What do you think you can do about that?" she cried.

Willa had nothing to say. She could only cry. Willa then ran upstairs to her bedroom and locked the door behind her. As she was running up the stairs, she heard her mom yell.

"So, what are you going to do about my hurt and pain? I thought you were going to help!"

Willa's head was swirling. "I don't understand. How could that have happened?" she thought, crying. "I was there last night to put the string on their doorstep, so God could help keep them from any harm." She didn't say a word about the string to anyone. She was too afraid they would blame her for the tragedy.

When she returned to school that Monday, she couldn't wait to talk to either Sister Mary Helen or Sister Mary Claire. Willa went to search for them because she had so many questions in her head. She felt as if she did not get them out, she would surely explode, but neither one of them was there on Monday. Willa did not know what to do. She needed her questions answered. Monday seemed to go by too slowly. It dragged on and on. Tuesday came by too slowly, and it couldn't get here fast enough. When the bell rang after school, Willa ran out of the class and to the church's basement. She needed to talk to one of the nuns NOW! Sister Mary Helen was in the bathroom when she got there.

"The entire Allen family died on Friday, the day after I went over to put the string on their porch. What happened? What went wrong? Did I do something wrong?" she blurted out the questions.

"You shouldn't question the works of God. It was too late to save them. They've sinned, there was nothing any of us could do for them. You did all you could do now be quiet and do what you're told, or the same thing can happen to your family. Is that what you want?" she asked.

"No, I don't want that to happen to my family," Willa answered.

When the other girls came in, they all sat around in the circle and talked. Willa found out that her neighbors were not the only ones who had sinned so bad that they could not be saved. The girls were all told to be quiet and to forget about what had happened. They were reminded that they were sworn to secrecy. The work they were doing was of God, and they didn't want to get him angry at them. Therefore, everyone agreed and obeyed. The girls were instructed to do the same thing to other families and the same thing kept happening. They would either all die, or their bones would get broken. Willa could not understand why so many families that went to church could sin so badly. Why couldn't God give them another chance at life?

Willa and her friends met at their clubhouse to discuss the events that were happening. It seemed as though instead of helping the people, they were killing or hurting them. Everybody who they chanted for and then went to go sell seasonal candies to, while they dropped the piece of string on their porch, was doomed somehow. They all were afraid to talk to their parents because of the oath they had taken to keep it a secret.

"Do not tell anyone, not even your parents." The words were clear; they had no one to tell except each other. The girls started a pact to get together at the clubhouse each time they put a string on somebody's porch. The day before they had to leave a string on a porch, they would say a prayer for the family, asking God to forgive their sins. The prayers never worked. All the people they prayed for were just too far gone in sin.

One evening after school, Willa and her friends met at the clubhouse to do some chanting for Elizabeth. She hadn't been to school for a week because she was sick. There was six girls who joined the secret club, but because Elizabeth had taken ill—now there were just the five. The girls all went into a trance, through meditation calling out to Lady Catherine. She came to them and instructed them to repeat a different chant. This time they were to put the string under Elizabeth's bedroom window instead of putting it on the front porch. Lady Catherine talked through Carmen this time since Sister Mary Claire wasn't around. This time was different; they immediately said a special prayer for Elizabeth's quick recovery.

"This time it should work," said Natalie. "We chanted different words. I think it's because we are asking for someone to get well soon because she is sick and not a sinner. In addition, this time we said a prayer together before going and dropping the string. Now we can all go to Elizabeth's house and leave it on her window sill," she added.

Three days had passed since they had their own secret meeting in the clubhouse. Friday arrived and they still had not heard anything from or about Elizabeth.

"I wonder how Elizabeth is doing?" Willa questioned the other girls during lunch hour.

"I don't know. When I passed her house this morning on my way to school, her house looked as if no one was even there. Maybe they went on vacation," Theresa said.

"Yea, maybe they went somewhere warm like Hawaii," Rebecca said, excited for Elizabeth.

Willa and the others made plans to meet in the clubhouse on Monday because Willa had to be at her Grandpa's house for the weekend. The clubhouse was at her house and there was no way the girls would go there without her, because they were all afraid of Esther.

Monday came and they all got together to go to the clubhouse. They wanted to ask Lady Catherine about Elizabeth. They figured that if anyone could give them any answers, she would be the only one to ask. They had to go about it this way because when they questioned either of the nuns, they were told to be quiet and mind their own business and there are just some questions that shouldn't be asked. Now above all, they now have to keep secrets from the nuns as well, because they went behind their back to summon Lady Catherine once, and now they were going to do it again. The girls all sat in a circle and started the meditation and chanting.

"Help me someone, please help me," Carmen was screaming.

They all opened their eyes to see Carmen's hair up in the air. It looked as if someone or something was pulling at it, but there was no one but them around her, and they were all holding hands.

"Stop that, Carmen. Quit playing around. You're scaring us," Theresa yelled.

"Help me, I swear, I'm not playing. Please help," Carmen screamed.

The girls all got up to help her. They tried pulling her hair back down, but whatever had hold of it, was not going to let go. Finally, whatever had hold of Carmen's hair let go and the girls all ran out of the room screaming. Whatever spirit they conjured up, wasn't happy with them and is now throwing things around. All of the girls were screaming and crying. They rushed Carmen into the house to rinse her head in the kitchen sink because she was bleeding from the experience in the clubhouse. When she put her head down, she glanced over to the toaster and saw the blood running down her face. She screamed louder than before, crying out of control.

Willa went running for her mom, screaming and telling her what had just happened.

"Carmen needs your help. She got her hair pulled out and is bleeding from her head. Come quick, she needs you," Willa cried hysterically.

Esther came running with her into the kitchen. By now there was a large amount of hair and blood in the sink.

"What is going on? What happened to her? What did you girls do to her?" Esther yelled.

"We didn't do this to her. We brought her in to help her," Willa cried.

"How did this happen? Who did this to her? She is not bleeding and losing her hair for nothing!" Esther screamed.

"We were just doing some meditation and chants to make Elizabeth feel better. We miss her and want her to come back to school. When she didn't come back, we decided to do some chants and that's when Carmen started screaming because she was getting her hair pulled out by something. We couldn't see who or what it was. Honestly, we didn't hurt her. It was something else," Willa tried explaining through her sobs.

"Jacob, go call the parents of these girls. Tell them it is an emergency, and they need to come quick," Esther blurted.

Esther stayed with Carmen. She made sure the bleeding stopped but there were many bald spots all over Carmen's head afterwards. When the other mother's came, they were shocked to see what had happened to Carmen. They asked the same questions Esther had already asked.

"There is something Willa was telling me. I wanted you all to be here to listen to what these girls have been doing in their 'so-called clubhouse.'" Esther said.

"Go on, Willa, tell them what you told me; why this happened to Carmen," She demanded.

"I can't. I'll get into trouble and we will all die," she cried.

"What do you mean? What are you talking about?" Esther roared.

"If I tell you, God will get angry at me and kill my whole family," she said.

Esther repeated everything Willa told her about the events that led up to this incident.

"Where did you girls learn to do this?" Mrs. Espinosa (Carmen's mom) asked.

"We learned to do it at school. Remember how we have to stay after on Tuesday and Thursday? That's when we learned," Darla said, eager to tell.

The parents were all shocked to hear what the girls had been doing on those days after school.

"I was told that Natalie was talented and gifted. They told me that she was going to stay after school to get special tutoring so she wouldn't lose interest. They said gifted children usually get bored since learning comes too easy to them," Mrs. Carlin (Natalie's mom) responded.

"So did we."

All the mothers nodded in agreement.

"What is going to happen to us? I told you what would happen if we told anyone," Willa asked nervously.

The parents all promised them that no harm would come to anyone as long as the truth was told. The girls then explained what they were doing with the neighbors, and how instead of making things better for them, the entire family would die or get hurt.

"Are we the ones who killed them?" Willa questioned. "Did we do the chanting wrong?" she added.

"No, none of you killed any of those people. What you did to them, however, is what killed them. You girls are innocent. You were told to do something you thought was right and the consequences were horrific," Mrs. Logan (Darla's mom) explained.

"What you girls are doing is witchcraft. Do any of you know what witchcraft is?" she asked.

The girls all shook their heads no.

"I don't know if I should tell you this, but here it is," Mrs. Carlin said. "Elizabeth died last week. She got pneumonia and there was nothing the doctors or anyone else could do," she explained.

"We killed her, didn't we? We killed her with witchcraft," Willa cried out.

"We never meant to hurt anyone; we thought we were helping them. Is God going to punish us for doing witchcraft?" Theresa asked.

"No, if you knew what you were doing, then he would punish you, but none of you knew what was really going on; that makes you innocent," Mrs. Espinosa assured them.

All the mothers agreed that taking the girls out of that school and putting them into public school would be better. They made a promise to the girls that they would not let anyone at the school know the real reason for them leaving the school. They explained to the Mother Superior that they thought it would help the girls academically—especially since they had a program equipped for gifted and talented children. They felt that would help the girls socially. Willa figured that neither Sister Mary Helen nor Sister Mary Claire ever found out about the girls and her telling what they did in the secret club—since none of the families of any of the five girls died. Willa never wanted anything to do with the Catholic religion again, but too bad for her. She had to go to church every Sunday with Grandpa and Vesta. She started having different dreams—ones that had her spinning on a large wheel.

Chapter Fourteen

When Willa was ten years old, she went to the zoo with Grandpa and Vesta. The day was fun and long, since they made sure to see all of the exhibits. That night she went to bed extremely tired from the long day. As soon as her head hit the pillow, she fell right to sleep. It seemed she had just closed her eyes when she suddenly woke up because the bed she was lying on started spinning. It went around and around, faster and faster, not to slow down.

"Oh, my God, what's happening? What's going on?"

Her first thought was to get out of bed, but when she opened her eyes to see what was going on, the walls and the furniture were all a blur. She saw that she was in a large, very well lit, empty concrete room. The ceiling seemed high, but it kept getting lower as she spun higher. Turning her head slowly to the side, she opens her eyes, hoping maybe it will help. She wanted all of this madness to stop. She was confused—not knowing where she was. She only knew that she wanted the spinning to stop. She wasn't at Grandpa's house anymore.

"What is going on? Where am I?"

She starts to lose control. All she can do is hang on and hope not to fly off hitting a wall. She tries to grab for something to hang onto, but there is nothing.

"What happened to the sheets?"

Thoughts are reeling in her head.

"They were here not more than a minute ago when I got into bed."

But a minute ago, she wasn't spinning, either.

She could feel the fear inside of her rising, Her heart is beating very rapidly, feeling as though it will beat right out of her body, the beating in her ears, sounding like there were soldiers marching within her. She could feel herself starting to hyper-ventilate. Her throat is dry and sticky and she was feeling terrified—scared that she is going to slide off the bed, which has now turned into a large flat spinning table. As the table is spinning, it is also rising up to the ceiling. "What is happening? Why am I rising up word on this table? Am I going to get crushed? Am I going to slide off? What is going to happen? How can I stop this? Thoughts were reeling through her brain. "I don't know!" she cries. "I don't even know how I got here." Help me, please, God. Come to me and help me. Get me out of here."

There is someone standing beside the table—a man whom she has never seen before. He is staring at her; waiting to grab her as soon as she flies off the table. He wants to take her soul. Somehow, she knows what he wants. "How do I know this?" she thinks. "How do I know what this man wants? Have I been here before?" She knows he cannot touch or hurt her while she is on the table, so he keeps pushing and spinning it faster and faster, because there is nothing for her to hold onto. When this all started, she remembers being bound by leather straps, but now they are gone; they just disappeared. With every turn of the wheel, her heart beats faster. She can feel the adrenaline rushing throughout her body, as the heat of her blood intensifies. She can hear the beating in her ears, and sees it pulsating in her chest. Her mouth is dry, and her throat is itchy; making it hard for her to yell for help. As she tries to yell, she starts to choke. All she can do is cry, hoping this will end. She is getting dizzy. Her stomach is now upset and making her nauseated.

"If the spinning doesn't stop soon, I am going to puke!" she screams.

She can see people standing all around—both inside and outside of the building she is in. The man who is standing beside the wheel—the one who keeps spinning it and laughing at her, suddenly speaks.

"Hi Willa, I've waited a long time for this—for you to come to me. Welcome to my castle," he said.

"Who are you? Why am I here? What do you want from me?" she cried.

Somehow, he was hovering over her and allowing her to see him at all times.

"Don't worry, you will find the answers to all of your questions soon enough."

She could see people standing all around her. Those who were on the outside were pounding on the window trying to come inside to help her. Somehow, she knows these people; even though she can't see their faces. She knows she can trust them. As they see her tears and hear her pleas for help, they try harder to get in.

"We will try our best to save you, Liliath. You won't spin off. Just hang in there and hold on tight," she heard the voices say.

"Liliath? My name isn't Liliath. Who are they talking to? They are looking at me," she thought.

"My name is Willa, not Liliath," she yelled through the pounding, banging, and the screams.

"Who are you trying to kid? Your soul will always tell the truth. You are truly Liliath," the man said.

Their fists were bloody from banging on the windows and the bricks.

"I wish they could help me," she cries.

But, not only are the windows too thick to break; they keep rising higher and higher above their heads making them harder to reach. Willa can see the people disappearing slowly.

She can hear herself yelling, "Help me! Please help me! I don't want to be here anymore!"

The few people who are inside the building are dressed in long black gowns with hoods to cover their heads. She looked to see if she could recognize anyone but she couldn't see their faces. It was as if they didn't have any. All she could see was a dark hole where a face should be and red glowing dots where their eyes should be. Like the man who is hovering, she can see him. She knows he's a man, but she cannot see his face.

"Help me, someone help me," she screams as the wheel seems to be spinning faster than before.

"Who are you?" she cries out to them. "What do you want? Why are you doing this to me?"

No one is listening. Maybe they can't hear, she thought. She knows she is screaming because she can hear herself. Somehow, however, it is all in her imagination. She realizes this because she cannot feel or see her mouth moving—she can only hear her voice.

She could feel herself slipping from the wheel.

"I'm slipping off. OH, GOD! Please save me!" she screamed at the top of her lungs. "Please stop this spinning, Lord! Wake me up! This is only a dream. It has to be. Please don't let it be real. I didn't do anything wrong. I was good. I wasn't bad. Please, God, let it be you who gets me when I fall. I can no longer hold on. If I am doomed to die, I want to go to heaven to be with you. Don't let him get me, whoever he is."

She sobs, feeling the heat of her tears. The wheel keeps rising up to the ceiling. She thinks she is going to get crushed. As she looks down at the people through the windows, she feels helpless.

"I am sorry for all my sins, Lord. When is this going to end?"

She is sobbing out of control, and feels as though she has been here forever, with no way out. She is starting to feel weak.

"I cannot hold on much longer. I feel myself sliding off the wheel."

She thinks, "Maybe I'll just die."

As she gives in, everything goes completely dark.

"Maybe I'll just die. Now I lay me down to sleep. I pray the Lord my soul to keep. If I should die before I wake, I pray the Lord my soul to take," were her last words before she got crushed.

Suddenly she feels the sheets. There is now something to hold onto. She grabs them because she is still spinning. She then wakes up and is sitting on the bed.

"Oh, my God, that was only a dream. I wasn't anywhere else. I was here all the time. I thought for sure I was going to die."

After that dream she was so terrified that she couldn't seem to go back to sleep, no matter how hard she tried. She stayed in the bed with her eyes closed and tried to get back to sleep. She tried to put good thoughts in her head, but because of the dream, she couldn't think of anything else. She looked around the room and made sure it was real. She recognized everything, so that told her she was fully awake, and not dreaming. The eerie feeling she had afterwards lingered on for days. She didn't understand what this dream meant or why it kept coming to haunt her. All she knew was that it scared her and she didn't want it anymore.

Chapter Fifteen

Willa started to have the nightmares at home in her own bedroom—
the place she stayed in for her sanctuary. The nightmares were all
different, yet they were all the same somehow. As she came up from
the cellar in Grandpa's house, feeling someone was watching her, she
held onto the railing and tried very hard to hurry up the stairs. She
could feel someone watching and waiting for her to let her guard
down, so they could pounce on her and tear out her flesh. She felt as
if they would eat her while she was still alive. She can't make it up the
stairs fast enough. There are things reaching out and grabbing at her.
They look like goblins, but they had the skin taken off their bodies,
making them look pink and bloody. She could see their veins standing
out and pulsating. As those things kept reaching out for her, she ran
up the stairs, trying to dodge them, and tried to stay away from them.
Her heart was pounding faster. Her adrenaline starts to flow, and the
beating of her heart is pounding in her ears. The further up the stairs
she gets, the more there are to climb. They seem to keep increasing
with every step she takes. Her legs are burning from the climb. She

feels hands grabbing and scratching her legs. They're pulling them and making it harder for her to lift them. Now the creatures are multiplying and are attacking her in all directions. She is getting tired and winded thinking there is no hope. She keeps running up and dodging them the best way she knows how. Finally reaching the top step, she finds the door is closed.

"Oh, God, please don't let this be happening to me. Help me get out of here!" she cried.

She pushed her whole body at the door to open it, but couldn't because the table ws against it to keep it shut. Someone or something pushed the table in front of the door to keep her locked in the cellar. She keeps pushing and pounding on the door and finally she gets it open. She can make a run for the front door, which it is at the other side of the house. As she tries to run through the kitchen, rats and mice are coming at her from the pantry. There is a man sitting there calling her to him

He tells her (without moving his lips), "Willa, come to me, Princess. Come here. It's okay. Don't worry, I'll take care of you," he says, trying to lure her.

"I don't know him, do I?" she thought. "Is it Grandpa?" She can't see his face. There is a bright light glowing inside the pantry window making it hard to see anything but a big dark figure sitting on one of the lower shelves. The mice are crawling on him and all around him.

"Is that you, Grandpa?" she cries.

But there is no answer to that question. He keeps calling her to him, and he wants her to go to into the pantry.

"Who are you?" she asks,

"Come in and see who I am," he says.

The voice doesn't sound like her Grandpa's voice but it sounds familiar.

She slowly moves toward him hoping he is her Grandpa. She knows he will help her get away from those things trying to grab at her from the cellar, and the rats and mice that are crawling around at her feet. Maybe he can help her get out of this house. She gets close enough to look at him. Then suddenly his face starts to melt, and blood is squirting out at her. He has no face left and there are only two glowing red dots where his eyes should be.

He starts to yell, "Willa, come, my Princess. Come and look into my eyes."

She tries to scream but she can't. It feels as though her throat is closing and she is losing her voice. He keeps calling her name.

"Willa, come to me. I will take care of you. Willa, I can help you. Come look into my eyes. You can trust me," he assures her.

He wants her to look into his eyes. What eyes? Why? There are only two red glowing dots where his eyes should be. At this point, she doesn't care who he is, or what he wants. She only wants to get out of the house. She was then able to scream. She turns around to run.

"I need to get out of here," she screamed.

Suddenly the windows in the pantry and the kitchen burst out with glass spraying all over. She has to duck and cover her face to avoid the debris. The wind is blowing so hard that it takes her breath away—making it hard for her to breathe. It is also pushing her back, and slowing her down. While the floor beneath her keeps crumbling under her feet, parts of the floor are soft and mushy like a big marshmallow. Her feet feel like they are running, but she is getting nowhere. Her legs and feet are moving so why can't she get anywhere? She keeps trying to run, no matter what the impediment may be. She tries as hard as she can to get out of there.

"I need to get out of this house," she keeps repeating in her head. As she passes through each room, the windows are flying at her, while the curtains are reaching out to grab her. They are trying to stop her from leaving the house. The wind is blowing so hard she can barely breathe.

"I have to get out of here! He can't have me, whoever he is. LORD, PLEASE give me the strength to go on. Help me to get out of this house," she cries.

As she is running, she can see and feel the mice all around her feet. They're making her stumble as she tries to run. She makes it a point not to look down anymore, because if she does, she will probably stop.

"I can't stop. I've come too far to give up and get caught," she sobs.

The fear of what it is that wants her, gave her the courage to keep going. What does that man want? What will happen to me if I stop? As she runs through the dining room, the window blows out and it flies at her and crashes on the wall behind her, barely missing her head. The curtains are growing. They are getting longer and now they are trying to reach for her from across the room. She can hear the telephone ringing. "Who could be calling? Is there someone on the phone who can help me? I can't go to the phone." There are those creatures from the cellar reaching in from where the window used to be, waiting for her to go near so they can grab her. The wind is now blowing harder and holding her back. It's keeping her from running out of the house. Everything everywhere is trying to keep her in this house. She is on her own. There is no one else around, and no one to help her. "Where is everybody?" the thought swirls in her mind. She reaches the hallway and the bathroom door is opening and slamming shut repeatedly, while a hand is reaching out from the bathroom closet to grab her. The floor beneath her is rising and tilting toward the bathroom, making her lose her balance to slide her into the bathroom. She tries to grab hold of the wall, but her fingers go through it. The walls on both sides of the hallway are now swelling, and are making it hard to get through. It feels like she is walking on marshmallows. She is sinking down with every step she takes. It is taking lots of effort to raise her legs again. "I don't think I am going to make it out of this house. I seem to be moving in slow motion. I know I will get caught moving this slow," she thinks.

"Help me, somebody help me, PLEASE!" she cries out.

She can feel the walls trying to crush her as she progresses through the hallway. She finally reaches the door to the bedroom and Grandma Emma is sitting on the bed. She is just staring at her. Grandma Emma is laughing at her. Her hand then reaches from across the room and out into the hallway at Willa. She could feel the cold rough touch of her hand grabbing at her ankle.

"OH, GOD, are you there? Can you hear me? Please help me. Don't let her get me, please," she cries. "Now I lay me down to sleep. I pray the Lord my soul to keep. If I should die before I wake, I pray the Lord my soul to take."

She repeated the prayer while choking on the words. She reaches down and grabs the hand, and pulls it from her ankle.

"I have to keep going. Don't look back. Just keep focusing on getting to the door."

The tears are burning her eyes and making it hard for her to see what is ahead. As she wipes them, she sees blood on the back of her hand. She starts to panic even more, because she is now bleeding from her eyes.

When she finally reaches the living room, it is the only peaceful place in this whole house. It seems so quiet, and so serene. She is so tired from what she has been going through, that she has to sit down on the couch to catch her breath. When suddenly out of nowhere, Ruby's body sits up and grabs her arm. Willa jumps up, trying to scream, but she couldn't. She lost her voice. Nothing would come out. Panic-stricken, she tries to run out of the room when the window comes flying out at her, and the curtains are reaching at her feet, making her trip, and fall to the ground. She quickly gets back onto her feet.

"I cannot be defeated. I have to keep going," she tells herself. In the front room, Grandma Emma's picture starts to swing slowly and then it starts swinging faster and faster while she is staring and laughing at her. The elk head above the fireplace is trying to get off the wall. It wants to attack her as well. This seems to be the hardest room to have to get through, because instead of the wind coming in at her side, it is now coming directly at her face. It's coming from both the window and the front door. It is getting harder to breathe. She keeps trying to gasp for air.

"Help me," she tries to scream, but can't.

"Is there anyone else in the world? Is there anyone who can hear me, besides the demons and evil in this house? Will I be rescued? The thoughts were reeling around and around in her head.

She sees herself getting closer to the front door. When she reaches it, she hears a voice telling her, "The only safe place for you to run to is the altar of the church that is sitting on the corner across the street."

"Will I finally find protection when I leave the house? Can I get across the street to the church? Will I finally be safe?" She is thinking and crying. "Where did this church come from anyway? It wasn't there before." She thought. It appeared from out of nowhere, but somehow, she knew it was going to be there. Fear made her wonder if it was safe to go into the church since this it was never there before. "I could barely make it out of the house. Now I have to run across the street and into that church?" she thought, exhausted.

Finally making it out of the house, Willa could feel the breath of all the demons on her neck. She could hear footsteps coming closer and closer. Not knowing or caring whose they were, she knew that she couldn't look back to see who or what it was that was chasing her. She didn't want to take any chance of slowing herself down. She kept on running. Finally, she made it out of the front door. She jumps off the porch, tripping, and she tumbled to the ground.

"I've got to get up!" she cries.

It is hard. She feels as though she can't get up. Suddenly she is too heavy for her arms, and unable to push herself back onto her feet. Her head is growing large, making it difficult for her to do anything.

"Lord, please help me! Lift me up!" she sobs.

The ground is turning into mush, making it hard for her to extend her arms, for the strength she needs to pull herself up. As she finally gets onto her feet, she runs across the street. Now the pavement is getting mushy and making it harder to run. It's allowing whatever it is that is chasing her, to get closer. She can hear and feel the breath of whatever it is on her neck.

"Don't look back. If you can't see it, it can't get you." "Looking back will only slow you down," she kept repeating to herself.

As she ran, birds came flying down and started pecking at her—mostly at her legs, making them weaker for her to run. The birds were pecking at her head and pulling her hair out. The church seemed to be getting closer just a few seconds ago, but now it seems to be moving away from her.

"I don't think I can reach it if it doesn't stop moving. I don't know if I'll have the strength to carry on. I have to keep going. I can't give up now," she thought. Looking up, she sees a window on the side of the church. There is a preacher standing at the altar in front of the pulpit, and a congregation of people are sitting in attendance listening to his sermon. She screams out for help, but no one moves. "They can't hear me," she thought, sobbing uncontrollably. She screamed louder, again no one heard.

"Just let me get to the church. Someone will help me," she cries.

When she finally reaches the steps of the church that leads to the front door, there he was, standing at the door—the man from the pantry.

He is calling me, "I've been waiting for you, Princess. What took you so long?" he laughed.

Willa turned around and ran to the alley on the side of the church. She found a back door. Upon entering the church, she starts to feel safer, and finally she can relax. No one can get her now; no one can harm her in here, in the house of God.

"I'm safe," she said, with a sigh.

Then the ceiling starts to crumble.

She can hear the voice telling her, "The only safe place for you to run to is at the altar."

She ran to the pulpit and sat inside in a fetal position. She covered her head, hoping she would be safe here. The walls were disintegrating. The church was falling apart, and she could feel the coldness of the wind at her back.

"Now I lay me down to sleep. I pray the Lord my soul to keep. If I should die before I wake, I pray the Lord my soul to take," she prayed.

She was hoping that her prayer would work, because it was the only one she could think of. The church has now crumbled down all around her. She can see the sky. It is bright blue with big beautiful white clouds. The man is standing just in front of the altar. The pulpit starts spinning and is trying to shoot her out of it. She realizes he can't get her while she is in here on the altar. She holds on as tight as she can. She finally gathers all of her strength and starts to scream louder and louder. She opens her eyes and the man is standing directly in front of her. Then his arms shoot out at her and grab her.

She sat straight up, looking around.

"I'm in my bed, in my own room," she thought, happy to know that she was safe. "It was only a dream."

She looked around to make sure she was safe, and that none of the evil that was in her dream had followed her out. She knew that it was a dream, but somehow she couldn't help but feel the horror inside of her.

"I don't want to go to sleep. What if I have the same dream? What if next time I can't stop dreaming and never wake up?" she thought. She was just glad her screaming didn't wake anybody up, especially her mom. Esther would be furious with her if she had awakened her. She turned around to look at the clock to see what time it was. It's only 3:00 a.m. —too early to wake up. "Should I take a chance in going back to sleep? Yes, I think I should. It's too scary sitting around in the dark," she thought. Willa fell back to sleep and had no other dreams. She woke up in the morning to the smell of bacon and hearing the birds chirping.

"I really am safe. I have nothing to worry about. Thank you, God, for giving me another chance to be alive," she prayed.

She got up, got dressed, and was now ready for another day.

Chapter Sixteen

When Willa was ten and one-half years old, she went to Grandpa's to spend two weeks of her summer vacation. Everything seemed so sunny all the time. She hadn't been having any nightmares. School had been great and she had no complaints about life in general. Everyday she would wake up, fold the sheets and blankets, and then put them neatly in the cubby of the couch. Then she would fold the bed back into its original form. She helped Vesta by vacuuming the front room and the living room. Then she dusted all the knick-knacks and wood. The house was always so clean and dust-free. They both got together one day and washed all of the windows; Willa washed the outside while Vesta did the inside.

A week went by and Vesta and Willa got along unusually well, even though both of them had to see each other all day long, everyday. When Willa was finished with her daily chores, she went outside to sit in the sun and pretend. She had no one else to play with because the neighborhood where Grandpa lived was mostly elderly people or young adults who were just starting a new life. Willa did miss her brothers, but mostly she was glad to be away from home. She has an active imagination, and she would sometimes pretend to be a princess, and Grandpa's house was the castle. Grandpa had built a fishpond in the back yard; in the warmer months, you could see the fish swimming around, but when it was cold outside, there was a tent to cover it up. Throughout the yard were huge walls made of bushes and vines. The only way to see in or out of the yard was through one of the two gates on either side. When you were in the back yard while the flowers were in bloom, it was a beautiful color show and the fragrance was mesmerizing. Willa loved being in the back yard. It was her fantasy land, and her time away from everything and everybody. Lunch was always at twelve noon, no earlier, and no later. Same with supper—it was always at five o'clock, no earlier or no later. That meant her make-believe world got interrupted during lunch and supper. During lunch, Willa could pretend that she was a princess. She secretly pretended to have a servant (Vesta), who catered to her needs. At suppertime, Willa's imagination saw Vesta as her evil stepmother and she was Cinderella. After everyone ate she had to clean the table and stove, wash and dry the dishes, and sweep the floor. Willa wasn't allowed to go outside after dark, which meant in the winter months, she had to stay in. However, after she finished her chores in the summer months, she was allowed to go sit on the front porch. The summer months could seem too long at times—it depended on what everyone was doing. Even though she couldn't see Ruby's old house from where she was sitting, she still felt uncomfortable being out there at times. She would start to remember that day she had found Ruby in her kitchen lying on the floor.

Toward the end of Willa's two-week stay on Thursday, it was a day she will always remember. She did her morning routine of folding the sheets and blankets, and then she folded up the couch. After breakfast, she went to clean up so she could do her chores. Willa started to go to the cleaning closet to get the vacuum cleaner.

"You can't go into the kitchen to get the vacuum cleaner," Vesta told her. "If you want to clean the rug, get down on your hands and knees, and lick it clean," she added.

Vesta was being extremely different from what she had been the past week and a half. She had been drinking that morning and was angry with Willa for reasons unknown.

Vesta started complaining to her, "You are always taking, and you don't think about others. When are you going to give something in return?" she yelled.

"I don't know what you want me to give to you, Vesta. I don't have anything. When I'm old enough to get a job, I'll give you money," Willa told her nervously, trying her best not to sound like she was getting smart with her.

"You ungrateful little bitch! I don't want your money. I don't want anything from you," Vesta screamed.

"What did I do wrong? What did I do to make you so angry?" Willa said, crying. "I don't know what you want from me, Vesta," she added.

"Don't get smart with me, you little princess bitch, or I will kick the shit out of you. I told you I don't want anything from you except my husband back, and it is far too long until Sunday night. Maybe you should pack your bags and leave now," she said, screaming.

Her eyes were glossy and red; they looked evil. Now more than before, Willa was scared to be there.

"I can't leave. Grandpa won't give me a ride home until Sunday night. Vesta. You know that," she cried.

Vesta lifted her arm and swung it back. Then she slapped Willa hard across her face. Everything turned dark and Willa lost her balance. She fell to the floor, hitting her head on the edge of the coffee table.

Vesta started yelling, "Now look at what you've done. Get up. You're getting blood all over my carpet."

She kept yelling and hitting her.

"I can't get up, Vesta. I am trying to, but I can't while you're hitting me," Willa cried. "Please, Vesta, it hurts. I can't get up. Please stop. I will go pack all my bags right now. I'll leave," she sobbed.

But Vesta kept punching her in the ribs and stomach so she wouldn't leave any visible marks. All along, she was yelling that she was going to kill her.

"Die, you little princess bitch, die. I am going to kill you and I'll laugh when I know you are in hell where you belong," she yelled.

Willa wished she could die, and then the pain would go away. She closed her eyes and silently prayed that this would all be over, and she could go home to be with God.

When Vesta was finished punching and kicking, she grabbed Willa by the hair to pick her up off the ground. Then she threw her down the hallway to the bathroom to get washed up. Each time Willa fell, Vesta would grab a handful of hair and pick her up, just to throw her down again. Willa was glad when they finally reached the bathroom because Vesta left her there alone. Willa ran the water in the bathtub, while she cried and wondered what it was that she had done wrong. What did she do to deserve the beating she just got? She tried not to cry. She tried to hold back the tears because she was afraid that Vesta would come in and hold her head under the water. But the tears wouldn't stop. She was hurt and confused.

"This vacation was going so good until today. What happened? I don't know what I did!"

Vesta came in to wash her hair. Willa told her she had already done it.

"I was able to do it myself," she said.

That made Vesta angry. She grabbed the bottle of shampoo and hit Willa on the head with it, before pouring any on her hair. Then she pulled her hair up to wash it. She just kept pulling it up and down, up and down.

"I wish this would stop. Please don't let me have anymore pain," Willa thought silently, trying not to show her pain to Vesta. She didn't want to make her angrier with her and try to drown her. She thought, "This time she may not give me the chance to live."

After Vesta finished washing Willa's hair, she got up and said, "Rinse it off yourself, you little bitch."

"Thank you, God," Willa thought, repeating those words in her mind over and over.

Willa finished taking her bath. She got out to dry off, making sure her back was turned toward the door. She didn't hear Vesta coming. Vesta hit her across the head with a bottle or something that was hard. Willa fell and hit her head on the sink. Her head started spinning and everything went dark. She was feeling nauseous. "Please, God, make her stop. If I was ever anything special to you, you would stop this pain and take me home to be with you," Willa prayed in silence.

"Get up! Quit pretending you're hurt. I didn't hit you that hard. Get up or I will really give you something to lay down and die for," she yelled.

Willa got up and the tears were running down her face. She was afraid to look at Vesta because she would see the tears and start hitting her again.

"I thought I told you to clean the blood off your face? Do you dare question my authority and go against my better judgment? Against my command?" she roared.

The blood she is seeing is new blood. I cleaned it off before I started bleeding again when she came in and hit her, when I hit my head on the sink, Willa was thinking.

"No, I thought I cleaned it. I'm sorry. I'll do a better job this time," Willa promised her, still crying and looking down at the floor.

"Look at me when I'm talking to you. Don't look at the floor. I am not lying on the fucking ground," she yelled as she started to get angry again.

Willa picked her head up and started sobbing.

"What have you done to yourself? Look at you! Your head is bleeding. Here, let me help you," Vesta said as she started crying.

She got a washrag and cleaned the blood off of Willa's face, trying to be as gentle as she could.

"What is going on here?" she thought. "What does she mean? I didn't do this to myself, she did it." Willa thought in silence, not saying a word. Willa stayed very still while Vesta washed the blood from her head and face.

After she was cleaned up, Willa went out to the back yard to play make-believe but she couldn't. She couldn't stop crying. She kept thinking of how her brothers had to go through all those times with Grandpa. Their punishment didn't last as long as hers, but they went through it numerous times and they got hurt. I don't feel good. Willa couldn't help thinking about what it was that got into Vesta. This was such a big change from all of last week, and the two of them were almost friends. "I don't want to be here anymore," she thought. Then she had thoughts of sneaking out of the yard and trying to find her way back home. "I've been back and forth plenty of times. I think I could remember the streets I need to go down," she thought. She tried to open the gate but it was locked. "I don't have the key! What am I going to do? Ask Vesta? No, I don't think so," she thought.

"I don't want to be here!" she said a little louder, hoping that maybe God couldn't hear her thoughts and that is why he didn't come to her rescue.

It didn't seem as if he heard her today.

Vesta called her to come in to eat lunch.

"Come in and eat some lunch," she said.

"I'm not hungry right now," Willa told her.

"You are much too skinny not to be eating. You need all the nutrition you can get, now come in and eat," Vesta insisted, her voice sounding like she was getting irritated.

Willa didn't want what happened to her earlier to happen again, so she got up and went in to eat. "I wish Vesta would choke on her food and die," she thought. She could never eat when she was upset and the food is too hard for her to digest when she is having anger problems. She still has a lump in her throat from all the crying she was doing. It made it hard for her to eat, but she had to get it down so she wouldn't upset Vesta again. She didn't want to go through the horror she went through this morning. Willa ate with her head down so Vesta wouldn't see the tears. As she ate, the tears kept dripping onto her sandwich, but she kept on eating because Vesta was sitting there watching to make sure she ate all her food. After lunch, Willa went back outside so she could sit alone and stay out of the house—out of Vesta's way.

When Grandpa arrived around four o'clock that afternoon, Willa was still in the back yard. She didn't go out to greet him even though she heard his car when he got home. He went out to the yard to announce his arrival from work. Willa turned a little, not wanting to look at him and waved. He came out to see what was wrong, and Willa was trying her hardest not to look up at him. But he lifted her face so he could see her. She couldn't help it. She thought all the tears were gone. She thought she couldn't cry anymore, but she started crying again. He was furious.

"Who did this to you?" he demanded.

Willa's face was bruised and she had a black eye.

"I tripped and fell on the coffee table, and then when I went to clean up, I fell and hit my head on the sink," she lied.

"I don't believe you. I can see a hand print across your face. I'm going to ask you again, 'Who did this to you?" he asked with a tight jaw. "I am not angry at you. You are not the one who is in trouble. Princess, I need to know. Tell me so I can take care of this."

He persuaded her as he was starting to turn red with anger, yet his voice sounded calmer that before. Willa knew he was very angry, and she couldn't answer him. She started crying harder than she was, because she had someone who could help her. However, she couldn't say anything, because no matter what Vesta did to her, she didn't want to see her getting hit.

He picked her up and took her into the house, yelling, "Vesta! Get over here, NOW!" he yelled. "Vesta, I said NOW!" he shouted.

Vesta came into the dining room where they were waiting and you could see that she had been crying.

"What's wrong?" she asked.

"Look at Willa's face! Just look at it. What happened to her?" he screamed.

"She was being bad. I had to punish her. She questioned my authority. She didn't do anything I asked of her. She was being a bad girl, and I just couldn't take it anymore. I didn't mean for it to go this far. I don't know what came over me," she cried.

"Is that true? Were you being a bad girl today, Princess?" he turned and asked Willa.

She shook her head 'no.'

"She just started hitting on me when I woke up this morning. I went to get the vacuum cleaner but she wouldn't let me. If I was being bad, I don't know what it is that I did," Willa explained.

Grandpa got up and started hitting Vesta, screaming and yelling, "How does it feel to get beat that badly?"

He started knocking her to the ground, making her hit her head on the furniture.

Vesta was pleading with him, "Please stop. I promise not to do it again. I don't know what got into me. I'm sorry, I didn't mean for this to happen," she begged.

Willa got up and begged Grandpa, "Please leave her alone. I'm better now, see?"

She showed him a smile to let him know she was okay with it now.

"I don't want to see her get hurt. Don't do this anymore, please," Willa begged.

Grandpa grabbed Willa into his arms and started crying. In her whole life, Willa had never seen Grandpa cry before. He didn't believe men should cry. He said it was a sign of weakness.

"Please forgive me. I never meant for you to get hurt so badly. I couldn't see the signs. You tried telling me numerous times, but I wouldn't listen to you," he cried.

He dried off his tears and said, "I am going to try my hardest to make the last three days of your visit a whole lot better. This I promise to you, Princess," he said.

Vesta got up and ran into the bedroom, slamming the door behind her. That evening, Grandpa and Willa went to pick up Chinese food for supper.

"Vesta is upset. I don't think she will want to cook tonight. Maybe we ought to surprise her and go pick up some dinner, what do you think?" he said.

It wasn't very often that Grandpa suggested going out to eat, so Willa jumped at the offer. Besides, she loves Chinese food.

"Okay, I'll go get my sweater, and then we can go," Willa said excitedly, glad that they were back to being a happy family.

All her bad thoughts that she had today were now gone. The day was over. When Grandpa and Willa returned with the food, Vesta brought out the TV trays and they all sat down to enjoy their food in the living room while they watched TV. During the meal, no one said a word. The dinner was delicious, but the atmosphere was cold. After everyone ate, Vesta and Willa cleaned up the mess and they continued the silence of the evening. At nine o'clock, it was bedtime. Tonight it was very inviting because of the coldness between the three all night.

"Goodnight Grandpa and Vesta," Willa said.

"Goodnight, Princess, I love you, too," Grandpa responded.

"Goodnight, I love you, too." A response came from Vesta as well, and then all of the lights went out

Willa slept very uncomfortable that night. She woke up early on Friday morning. She is usually sleeping when Grandpa is getting ready for work. She laid still so no one knew she was awake. She was thinking that maybe she could sneak out the front door after Grandpa left for work. She didn't know if Vesta went back to bed when he left, or if she stayed awake, because she usually didn't wake up until 7:30 a.m.. It was still dark in the house and the only light shining was the one from the kitchen. She heard Grandpa and Vesta talking, but she couldn't hear about what because they kept their voices low. Willa saw the kitchen light go off. She turned onto her side and closed her eyes, pretending to be asleep.

She heard Grandpa tell Vesta, "I'll see what I can do about getting home early today, so the three of us can go do something this afternoon, okay?"

"Okay, we will be waiting," Vesta told him, sounding happy.

Grandpa leaned down and kissed Willa's head.

Then he said, "God be with you today, Princess. I love you."

He turned to look at Vesta and said, "Make sure she has a better day than the one she had yesterday."

"I will. We will be pretty busy today," She assured him.

Then Willa heard the door open and shut. She could hear the car start and then she heard him drive away. The house was still dark, and the lights were still off, but the TV went on. "Oh no," she thought. "How am I going to sneak out of the house with Vesta sitting in the next room watching TV? I can't do it now." Willa got up acting like she just woke up.

"What are you doing up so early" Vesta asked.

"I guess it got cold through the night because I need to go to the bathroom," Willa lied.

She walked past Vesta like a scared puppy. Willa was afraid that Vesta would get angry with her for needing to go pee, but she just sat watching TV. Willa went to the bathroom and was in there longer than usual, grooming herself slowly. Her head was hurting more than it did yesterday, and she was being careful not to brush over the bumps.

Vesta hollered in the door, "Are you all right? You've been in there for awhile."

"Yes, I'm just finishing brushing my teeth," Willa yelled back.

She finally finished. Then she walked back to fold the sheets and blankets, and then she folded the bed back into a couch.

Willa went to the kitchen's cleaning closet in the back porch to get the vacuum so she could finish her chores early. She figured that if she got them done early, she could plan her escape. Vesta went into the kitchen and started frying bacon for their breakfast. Neither of them said a word to each other. Willa went into the front room and started vacuuming, thinking of the previous day. "What a horrible day it was. I never want to go through that again," she thought feeling anger toward Vesta. She finished in that room and then went on to the living room. All along, she thought about what had happened to her yesterday. Before she knew it, both rooms had been vacuumed. She started to wrap the cord up when Vesta called her.

"Leave your chores until after breakfast; it's time to eat now," she said.

"I'm done with the vacuum cleaner. I am wrapping the cord up. Should I finish and bring it with me when I go into the kitchen?" Willa questioned.

"No! Leave it there. Come in and eat before your food gets cold," she said with an irritated voice.

Willa left everything as it was and hurried to the kitchen. She noticed as she hurried past the bedroom that the door was slightly opened. She glanced quickly into the bedroom as she passed by. The bed wasn't made, but there was something peculiar about it; not knowing what it was that seemed strange. "Oh well, why worry about it. Whatever it is must not be very important. Willa sat at the table trying to eat her breakfast. She wasn't feeling hungry because of the bad thoughts that were in her head while she was vacuuming. She knew she had to eat or get into trouble, so she chose to eat.

After the two of them had eaten, Vesta asked, "Would you be a dear and wash the dishes so I could go get out of these night clothes and get dressed into something more presentable and make my bed. I haven't done that yet."

Willa agreed and started washing the dishes. Out of nowhere, she started to feel scared. The hair on her body was standing on end and the butterflies were fluttering around inside of her belly. "Vesta is up to something," she thought. She went back in her mind about when she passed the bedroom and the bed, wondering what was on it. Why did it seem so strange to her? "Just calm down. Don't worry, you will be out of here sooner than you think," she thought.

Willa's plan was to tell Vesta that she wanted to sit on the front porch today instead of going out back. Willa was allowed to go across the street to the little corner grocery store. "I can tell her I'm going to go buy me some candy or a soda or something," she thought. She finished drying and then put away the dishes. All along, she couldn't get over the feeling of the butterflies inside of her, or the feeling that she saw something strange in the bedroom on the bed. The more she thought about it, the more she started to think she somehow knew what it was. But she really didn't know because she didn't quite see what it was. Willa went into the living room to finish putting the vacuum away, and then went on to do the dusting. "I need to get these chores done," she thought. "I have to get out of here. I don't want to be here anymore. I want to go home." Tears started to roll down her cheeks. When Vesta came out of the bedroom, she sat down on her chair by the window to have a cigarette. Willa wiped the tears from her face.

She turned and asked, "When I finish dusting, could I go to Tom's (the little store) to get me something? I want to go for a walk and get some fresh air."

"Tom's isn't open yet. He doesn't open until nine o'clock. Isn't there anything else you could be doing for a half hour?" she asked.

"I guess I could go out back and color for awhile. Could you let me know when it's nine o'clock?" Willa asked.

"Sure, no problem," Vesta said.

Then Willa gathered up her coloring books and crayons and went outside.

While Willa was coloring, she must have forgotten about everything, because when Vesta came out to tell her the time, she noticed how many pages she had colored. There was a lot. Maybe the time went so slowly because Willa was expecting something, expecting to go to the store. Then when she was out of sight, she could sneak off to find her way home. As she gathered up all of her stuff she was thinking, "Maybe I shouldn't run away. Grandpa would be worried and I don't want to do that to him. Or what if I get lost and there are kidnappers out in the middle of the day waiting for a lost little girl to go by. I don't know what I want now, but I am too afraid to stay here," she thought as tears were rolling down her face.

"Willa, come in here. Your mom is on the phone, and she wants to talk to you," Vesta yelled out from the door.

"Okay, I'm coming," Willa said excitedly, wiping the tears away and grabbing her crayons and coloring books to go inside. She was thinking that the phone call was to tell her that her mom was going to come and get her. Now she doesn't have to run away.

"Hello."

"Hi, Willa, this is mom. I called to let you know that I called Grandpa at work and I talked to Vesta. Jacob and I have to leave on a trip out of town and the boys are going to stay at Uncle Tony's house until we get back. It shouldn't be longer than a week. I just wanted to let you know that you will be staying over there for another week."

Willa's heart dropped, and she started crying.

"I didn't bring enough clothes to stay for another week," she cried, hoping that her mom would change her mind.

"You have plenty of clothes there. You can wash them and wear them again. I guess we could go take you some more. Is there anything else you want out of your bedroom?" she asked.

Willa thought, "I hate her, why is she acting like she cares about me now?"

"No, I guess I have everything I need here," she said.

Willa wanted so much to tell her mom what went on here yesterday and she didn't want to stay here anymore. She couldn't tell because not only was Vesta standing and listening, but Willa didn't want to be the blame for messing up Esther's trip to wherever she was going. Maybe she knows, but doesn't care that she is hurting and scared. There went her plans to walk home—her world was falling apart. She didn't know if worrying about the kidnappers or worrying about Vesta was worse. She doesn't have to worry anymore about the kidnappers, since she can't go home now. Willa wanted to ask her if it would be okay that she stayed home by herself. She is old enough to take care of herself, and she doesn't need anyone to be there to feed her, because she can make her own meals. However, the words just couldn't come out. She just cried.

When Grandpa came home that afternoon around two o'clock, he asked, "Did you hear the good news? You get to stay here another week. Isn't that great, Princess?" he asked, his eyes glowing with joy.

"Yes, my mom called me this morning before lunch to tell me the good news. I was kind of disappointed at first, but I really do want to stay another week with you and Vesta. I think we can have a lot of fun together," she lied while crying.

"What's wrong, Princess? Don't worry we will have a lot of fun, I promise," he assured her while he was holding her.

She looked at him and nodded but the tears wouldn't stop. Willa didn't want to hurt his feelings. He seemed so happy over the news of her staying another week, but what she really wanted to blurt out was, "Look at me, Grandpa. I am bruised all over. Do you honestly think for one minute that I would want to stay another week here with that bitch you call a wife? I can't stand her just as much as she can't stand me. I really wish I had the strength to kick her ass like she done to me." Willa wished she would say those words to him. She vowed that one day when she was old enough, she would say those words—then let them try to do something to her.

Esther and Jacob brought Willa some clothes like promised, and also Willa got her very first Barbie doll. She wasn't allowed to have one before because the doll was anatomically correct. Getting the Barbie doll was the best thing that happened so far in the last couple of weeks. Not only did she get the doll, but she also got three other outfits to dress her in. Willa went outside to sit on the front porch to play with her new doll, but she could hear the conversation inside.

"What happened to her? Why is her face bruised and she has a black eye!" Esther asked with concern.

"She and Vesta had a disagreement, but I took care of everything. Don't worry, it won't happen again," he assured her.

While they all talked inside, Jacob came out to the porch where Willa was playing.

"Are you okay?" he asked looking at the black eye and the bruises.

"Yea, why?" she was curious; it didn't seem to matter to anyone else why is he concerned.

"I don't like what I'm looking at; your face is really bad," he said.

Then the tears came again. She started to feel sorry for herself again.

"We really don't have to go if you're not feeling comfortable staying here," he said concerned.

"It's okay, if you and Mom don't go because I said something she will make sure my life would be miserable. Go ahead and have fun. I don't think this will happen again," she assured him.

Esther and Jacob said good-bye and then they left. As Willa saw them drive away, she felt so all alone. Although Grandpa and Vesta were here with her, at that particular moment, she felt she was alone in this world, and the tears couldn't stop flowing. She wanted to chase the car, running and begging them, "Don't go. Please don't go. Don't leave me here all alone." She couldn't do that so she sat on the porch with her new doll, crying silently and watching as the car disappeared.

Chapter Seventeen

Things went well over the weekend. They stayed home because Willa's face was still bruised and her left eye was still black. Grandpa thought it would be better that Willa didn't go out in public because of the stares she would get from rude and nosy people. She was happy sitting in the back yard and playing with her new doll, dressing her up in the different outfits. Willa enjoyed the summer breezes and the wonderful smell that came from all around the garden. She was back in her fantasy world and when she is there, nothing or no one could bother her.

The weekend came and went. Grandpa had to go back to work. Vesta woke Willa up at 7:30 that morning. No matter how much Willa didn't want to be there at times, she loved waking up at that house—the smell of breakfast cooking every morning made it seem so inviting. At home, however, the only smell in the morning was coffee. Everyone had to serve themselves a bowl of cereal or make their own toast if they were hungry. There were exceptions, however. On the weekends, Esther did cook a big breakfast and also when there was company staying over.

"Get up and do what you have to do, I'm cooking breakfast. It should be done soon," Vesta said.

Willa got up and folded the blankets, sheets and the bed into a couch. As she walked to the bathroom, again she noticed the bedroom door open. The bed was messed up and there was something on the bed. At first, it looked like a person was still laying down, but who could it be? Grandpa went to work everyday no matter how he was feeling. Willa kept on walking to the bathroom, and she got cleaned up.

"Willa, are you almost done?" Vesta yelled.

"Yea, I'm finishing up right now. I'll be out in a couple of seconds," Willa yelled back.

"Okay, the food will be ready in a couple of seconds. Try to hurry," Vesta said in a happy voice.

While getting dressed, cleaning up, and combing her hair, Willa heard the birds happily chirping outside and the sun was shining bright in the house. The day was beautiful. Willa didn't trust it, because through her experiences, when the day starts out like this beautiful day, it meant something was bound to go wrong. Willa finished up in the bathroom and then went into the kitchen to eat her breakfast.

"Is Grandpa home today?" she asked Vesta.

"No, you know he goes to work on Monday. Why do you ask?" Vesta questioned.

"I was curious, because when I passed your room I couldn't help but notice the door was opened. When I glanced in, it looked like someone was still in bed and I knew it wasn't you," Willa explained. "I really wasn't trying to be nosy. It was just a quick glance, that's all," she added.

"No, there is no one in my bed. I just haven't made it yet. I figured I would wait until after breakfast to get it done. Nobody ever comes over this early to visit anyway," Vesta explained.

"The food smells so good. I love the way you cook, Vesta. The bacon is crisp just the way I like it," Willa said, trying to make peaceful conversation.

"Thank you. I notice what you eat most, so I try to make that more often because you're too skinny. Your Grandpa and I like to see you eat," she said.

That was the end of their conversation, while they ate.

When they finished eating, Vesta asked, "Will you clean up the mess? I really need to go in and fix the bed and change into some real clothes."

"Sure, I'll do that, no problem," Willa told her.

She cleaned the table and the stove. Then she swept the floor, washed, dried and put away the dishes.

After she was done, Willa went to the cleaning closet to get the vacuum cleaner. Then she started her journey to the front room to do her chores. As she walked down the hallway, Vesta came walking out of her bedroom closing the door behind her.

"You look pretty today, Vesta. Are you going somewhere?" Willa commented.

"I thought that after we finish our chores, you and I could go downtown to Grant's and do some shopping. There are a couple of birthday gifts I have to get, and I thought maybe you might want to get out of the house since your face has pretty much cleared up. You can help me pick the gifts," she said.

"I would love to go," Willa said excited.

"Good, it's a date. Maybe we can go eat lunch at a restaurant for a change," she said.

Willa was excited about going somewhere and doing something fun with Vesta. "Wow, what a change. Vesta wants me to go downtown with her and she wants me to help her pick gifts," she thought excitedly. As she continued to vacuum and dust, her mind was reeling with thoughts. "I don't know if it's a good idea to go with her. What if she tries to throw me in front of a car? No! Quit thinking like that. Vesta wouldn't do anything like that. Besides, there is no way I am going to stay in this house all alone. With a day like today, I know something bad will happen here, and I don't want to have to be alone to face whatever it is." She hurried to get her chores done. She was excited about going somewhere and not having to stay in the house all day with Vesta, even though she had her Barbie doll to play with. It wasn't the same as going somewhere else. Willa has never been downtown, but she has heard so much about it. She is very excited that she is finally going to go. Willa finished with her chores, put away the vacuum and cleaning stuff, and patiently waited for Vesta to finish.

"Have you ever ridden on the city bus?" Vesta asked.

"No, this will be my first time. It is also going to be my first time to go downtown. I've never been there before. I am so excited, and I can hardly wait," Willa said, her eyes shining so bright with excitement.

"Well then let's go. The bus should be at the stop any minute now. We don't want to miss it," Vesta said, smiling.

Vesta and Willa walked across the street to the bus stop that was in front of Tom's grocery store. When the bus arrived, they boarded, found a place to sit, and sat down. Willa got to sit next to the window. She looked out of it and watched as the world went by, making lots of stops on the way to pick up other people. As they got closer to their destination, the buildings grew taller than Willa had ever seen. She had been to the mall but in comparison this was far more exciting.

When they got off the bus at their stop, Vesta said, "Make sure you stay by me at all times. I don't want you to get lost."

Willa looked all around at the tall buildings and all the people; there were so many of them. They walked into Grant's department store because Vesta wanted to hurry to get the gifts and get out as soon as possible.

"See why I don't like coming downtown?" she asked Willa while looking around at all the people. "There are just too many people here," she added.

"I think it's exciting seeing all these people. Makes me wonder what everyone is doing here," Willa said.

"This time of the year, everybody is busy buying wedding gifts or birthday gifts. It's as if Christmas never passed, or if it is just around the corner any day now," Vesta explained.

Vesta and Willa looked through the clothes for a gift for her friend. "Vesta has a friend?" Willa wondered. The thought of that made her curious. She had never seen anyone come visit her, nor has Vesta ever gone anywhere to visit anyone. What would a friend of Vesta's look like? Willa shuddered to think of it. Vesta finally picked out a blouse for her friend; she didn't want to stay in this store.

"Let's go to the May Company after I pay for this," she said.

"Okay," Willa agreed.

They walked the six blocks to the May Company. There were even more people walking on the sidewalk. It was not as crowded as she had seen in movies, but there were more people than she could have ever imagined being in one place. The present Vesta wanted to buy at the May Company was to Willa's surprise again. It was for Vesta's daughter. "What! Vesta has a daughter? I never heard this one before. I am sure that I would have heard about someone as important as a daughter," Willa thought.

"I didn't know you have a daughter, Vesta," Willa told her.

"You didn't? Your mother knows my daughter. Her name is Clara. Your mom and she were best friends at one time. That is how I met your Grandpa was through Clara," Vesta explained.

"My mom never told me about her. This is the first time hearing about your daughter," Willa said.

"Clara is a few years older than your mom and she has children who are a little older than you kids," Vesta went on to explain.

Wow, what a shock! Willa couldn't get over the fact that Vesta is a mother, and not only is she a mother, but there are children also.

"Why haven't they come to visit anytime I was there? Have they ever been to your house to visit?" Willa questioned.

"Yes, they have been to visit me. Why are you asking all these questions? It is really none of your business," Vesta snapped, and started to sound aggravated.

Willa stopped asking questions so she wouldn't get Vesta angry. They looked all around on the racks, and then Vesta picked a blouse and a pair of pants for Clara. Then they went to pay for them.

"Are you hungry?" Vesta asked. "It's pretty close to lunch time," she said, looking at her watch. "It's a quarter 'til twelve," she said.

"Sure, where are we going to go eat?" Willa asked as they were walking.

"Come on, we'll go in here and eat," she said about a bar sitting on a corner.

"It's a bar," Willa said. "I don't think we should go in there. They might not have food in there," she added.

"Look at the sign. If you would pay better attention, you can see it is a restaurant and bar. They have food here," she said pointing at the sign.

"Okay, I guess it will be all right," Willa said giving permission to enter.

Willa wondered why Vesta was asking her permission to eat there. She is the adult and has never asked Willa for her opinion before today. They were seated at a booth and given a menu. The waitress asked if they wanted anything to drink and Vesta ordered herself a Seagram's VO and a tonic, and Willa ordered a coke.

While they were looking at the menu, Willa asked, "Is Clara your only child?" trying to break the ice.

"Yes, I only have one," she answered.

"How many children does she have?" Willa questioned.

"She has three boys. Why do you want to know?" Vesta said.

"I don't know, I guess I am just curious to know about my other family," Willa went on. "How old are they?"

The questions wouldn't stop.

"Her oldest son is named Anthony, and he is sixteen years old. Then there is Hector, who is twelve years old, and the youngest is Raymond. He is ten years old," she said.

Willa wondered if Vesta treats them nice or if she hates them, too.

"Am I going to meet your daughter and grandchildren Vesta?" Willa was curious.

"Yes, they will be over to the house on Wednesday. What is this? Twenty questions?" she said.

"No, I guess I'm just curious, because this is the first time I've ever heard about your daughter, Clara and your grandsons. I really didn't mean to pry," she explained.

The waitress came back with their drinks and they ordered their lunch. Vesta finished her drink and ordered another one. They ate in silence and when they finished they went to the bus stop, got on the bus and went back home. Willa had a fun day with Vesta. It didn't turn into a disaster like she thought it would, even though the birds were chirping and the sun was shining brightly. The rest of Monday and Tuesday seemed to go by too slowly. Willa was too excited knowing she was going to meet Vesta's daughter and her grandsons.

On Wednesday, Willa was too excited. She woke up early, even before Grandpa left for work. She wanted to get her chores done early and wait for the arrival of the company.

"What are you doing up so early, Princess?" Grandpa asked.

"I couldn't sleep. I wanted to get up early to get my chores done. I didn't want to oversleep today," she explained.

"Well, I am glad to see you are so enthused. What brought that on?" he asked.

Vesta was standing behind him and looked at Willa. Willa saw that she was shaking her head no. She knew at that point that she shouldn't say anything about Clara and her sons coming over.

"I don't know why, I just woke up feeling excited today." She covered up.

"Well, it's six o'clock. I better get out of here, and there is a lot of work to be done today," he told them.

Vesta handed him his lunch box and gave him a kiss on the cheek.

"God be with you today, Princess. I love you. Remember to have a good day," Grandpa told Willa, and not saying a word to Vesta.

He gave Willa a kiss on the forehead, and then walked to the front door to leave. "He did it again, and this time I'm awake. He kissed me and told me, "May God be with you. I guess he does this everyday, she thought. "Maybe this is the reason Vesta gets so jealous. He kisses me and not her. He talks to me and not her. It's not my fault, I am usually asleep when he does it," she thought.

"Bye, Grandpa, I love you, too," Willa told him.

Then he closed the door and Willa heard him drive away.

"Wasn't I supposed to say anything about Clara and her sons coming over for a visit today?" Willa asked Vesta.

"Your Grandpa doesn't like Clara; he doesn't allow her being in this house. She usually has to sneak over to see me," Vesta explained, looking sad.

"I'm sorry, Vesta, maybe we can talk to him about it, and maybe we can change his mind," Willa said, trying to make Vesta feel better.

"No, the best thing is to keep the visits quiet. I don't want to get him angered," Vesta said sadly. "So, what do you want for breakfast?" she said, cheerfully changing the subject.

All of the times Willa spent at Grandpa's and Vesta's house, Willa had never known that Vesta got up so early in the morning to cook breakfast for Grandpa, until that morning. She had noticed before that there had been an extra plate when she washed the dishes, but it never dawned on her that Grandpa ate breakfast so early in the morning.

"I could eat some cereal, that way you don't have to cook and there won't be so many dishes to be washed. We could have our chores done by the time Clara and her sons come over," Willa suggested.

"They won't be over until around 11:30. We have plenty of time," she said.

Willa served herself a bowl of cereal and ate, while Vesta went to the bedroom to get dressed and fix her bed. Without being told to, Willa finished eating. Then she cleaned up the kitchen and washed, dried and put the dishes away. Then she went and got the vacuum cleaner, the furniture polish, and cleaning rags. She hurried to do her chores, so Clara and her sons could visit in a clean house. It was such a warm day, so Vesta went around the house and opened all the windows to get that cool early morning breeze. It was such a lovely day, and Vesta even got out a record and played music while they cleaned. Before long, the house was spotless.

Eleven o'clock was coming close and Willa was getting antsy. She couldn't keep still. She wanted to meet Vesta's family. At eleven o'clock, Willa was in the kitchen getting a drink of water when she heard the doorbell ring. She almost spilled it all over herself.

"Oh, my God, it's probably them," she thought. She wiped herself with the dishtowel, then went to the living room and sat down like a good girl should. Vesta let a lady and her three kids in, and kissed each one in the doorway. Vesta was crying and it made Willa almost start to cry. Willa was so happy for her.

"Come in, come in. We can't stay here in the doorway. Come and sit down. How was the drive out here?" Vesta asked Clara.

"It was fine; it's not that long of a drive, Mother. I only live ten minutes away," Clara told her. Clara was nothing like Willa imagined her to be. She was actually very beautiful and young looking. If she and Esther were friends, Clara must have been a lot younger, because she looks so young. She has beautiful black hair that is shiny; her eyes are dark and they seem to have a glow. She is thin, almost like a model. Willa couldn't believe that this was Vesta's daughter. They look nothing alike.

"I want you to meet Carl's granddaughter. This is Willa. Willa, this is my daughter, Clara, and these are her three sons—Tony, Hector and Raymond," she said, introducing them.

"Glad to meet you," Willa told them.

"Glad to meet you, too," they all said together.

Tony is somewhat tall and skinny, and he is funny looking. He reminded Willa of Howdy Doody with his bright orange hair and the freckles all over his face. Hector looks more like his mom with his dark hair and big brown eyes; Willa thinks he is kind of cute. Raymond is dark skinned with dark curly hair and big round dark eyes. None of the brothers looked like one another.

"Willa, why don't you take the boys out to the back yard to play, while me and Clara sit and talk for awhile? We have a lot of catching up to do," Vesta asked.

"We can go out to play; I don't have any toys here that you can play with," Willa informed them. "What do you want to do?" Willa asked them.

"I don't know," they all said together.

"Vesta, can we go to the store first before going out to the back yard?" Willa asked. "I have some money. I can buy the guys a pop and some candy," she added.

"You can go get that stuff but you have to leave it with me because I'm going to start lunch in a few minutes," Vista told Willa.

"Okay," Willa replied.

Then she turned to the boys and asked, "Do you want to go to the store? It's only across the street," she said to them.

"Sure," Tony said.

They all went to the store.

"Hi, Tom, how are you today?" Willa asked the storeowner.

"Hi, Willa, how is the little Princess?" Tom asked her.

"I'm fine, I would like you to meet..." she stalled for a second and then turned around and looked at them wondering what to refer to them as. "My cousins, I think they are my cousins. They are Vesta's grandsons; this is Tony, Hector, and Raymond," Willa informed him while pointing at each one as she said his name.

"Glad to meet you," Tom said to the boys.

"Glad to meet you, too," they all said together.

Willa thought, "Gee do they always say things together?" They finished getting the things at the store, and then went back to the house and gave Vesta the goodies. Then they went out to the back yard to play until they were called in for lunch.

"What do you want to do?" Willa asked, looking at all three of them.

"I don't know," Tony said, all alone this time.

"Why don't you come over more often?" Willa asked.

"My mom only comes on birthdays and just before Christmas; she doesn't like coming to visit Grandma," Tony informed her.

"Why, what's wrong with visiting her?" Willa asked being curious.

"I don't really know that much, but your Grandpa doesn't like my mom because he says she's a whore and he doesn't want any whores in his house," Tony said.

"I'm sorry, I didn't know. Maybe I shouldn't have asked," Willa said feeling bad for them.

"It's okay; I don't mind telling you, since we are sort of cousins," Tony said.

"Vesta never told me that she had any grandchildren. I didn't know until yesterday," she said.

"She and my mom stay away from each other as much as possible because Grandma said 'It's okay for mom to come visit, but try to get a sitter for us.' She says she doesn't want us to dirty up her house," Tony told her.

"I know how Vesta is, she hates me," Willa told him.

"I know, my mom told us about that," he said.

"Why does Grandpa call your mom a whore?" Willa questioned.

"Because he says the reason why we have different dads is because my mom likes to sleep around with every Tom, Dick, and Harry. It's just that every time my mom thought she found Mr. Right, he would beat her up and then leave her. It's not her fault, really," Tony said, giving Willa more information than she asked for.

"I'm sorry, it must be hard for you," she said sympathetically.

"Not really, I don't need a father. I have friends who have their dad and they get beat up by him. I can do without that," he said. Willa and Tony talked for a long time while the other two were playing at the other end of the yard. Willa got more information than she could ever imagine. For instance, she didn't know Vesta was a prostitute and Grandpa Carl used to pay her for sex. Then he took her off the streets and married her. She left her daughter to fend for herself when she was a young woman. That's why Clara made so many mistakes in her life.

Vesta called them in to go have lunch. They all sat down at the dining room table instead of eating in the kitchen. Another first for Willa. They never sat at that table as long as she could remember.

"How old are you, I can't remember your name?" Clara asked, looking at Willa.

"My name is Willa and I'm ten and a-half years old, but I will be eleven years old in July," Willa answered.

"So you are Esther's daughter?" she asked.

"Yes," Willa answered.

"How is your mom?" Clara asked.

"She's doing okay; she went on a trip so I guess she's having a lot of fun right now," Willa said.

"You are awfully small for your age. You are so tiny," Clara said.

"Yea, everyone tells me that. They don't believe my age when I tell them how old I am," Willa said.

"Where are your brothers, are they with an uncle or aunt?" Another question from Clara.

"Yes, they are staying with my uncle Tony until she gets back," Willa informed her.

"Did you know that your mom and I used to be best friends?" she asked Willa.

"Yes, sort of. Vesta was telling me about it yesterday," Willa told her.

"I'll give you my phone number so you can give it to your mom. Tell her to give me a call sometime. I've asked mother here to do me that favor, but she can never seem to remember to do it. Will you do that for me?" she asked Willa.

"Sure, I'll give it to her. Can I keep it, too? So I can keep in touch with your sons since we are sort of cousins?' Willa asked.

"Sure, maybe we can all get together someday and visit for awhile and get to know each other. How does that sound?" she asked Willa.

"I think it sounds great. I think my mom would like seeing you again," Willa told her.

Clara wrote her phone number on a piece of paper, then folded it and put it in Willa's purse.

They all finished eating lunch.

"Well, I hate to eat and run, but I have things to do before it gets too late. Thank you for the present, mother," Clara told Vesta.

She looked at Willa and said, "Don't forget to give your mom my phone number, okay? It was very nice meeting you. Sorry we can't stay longer to get to know one another better, but there will be another time," she said.

"Goodbye," Willa told them as they walked out of the door.

"Goodbye," they all repeated together.

Vesta and Willa watched them from the screen door as they disappeared.

Vesta turned, looked at Willa, and said, "Don't forget, this is our secret. You must not tell your Grandpa that we had any visitors today."

"I won't. I'll keep my mouth shut," Willa promised.

CHAPTER EIGHTEEN

For the next two days, things went smoothly. Willa never told the secret to Grandpa. He will never know that Vesta had her daughter and grandsons over for a visit. It was a very quiet couple of days, and Willa was glad that things were going pretty smooth. The phone rang and Vesta got up to go answer it.

"Willa, it's for you," she shouted.

Willa got up to go answer it. She thought it was her mom calling to tell her she was going to be gone another week and now she was dreading to answer the phone.

"Hello," Willa said to the person on the other end.

"Remember me?" the voice on the other end asked.

"I'm sorry, no I don't recognize your voice," she told him.

"It's Tony, Vesta's grandson," he said.

"Oh, hi. How are you?" Willa asked, glad that it was him on the phone and not her mom.

She was surprised he called, and she wasn't expecting it.

"I'm okay, what are you doing?" he asked.

"Nothing, I was just sitting in the living room playing with my Barbie doll," she admitted. "What made you decide to call me?" Willa was curious to know.

"I don't know, I thought maybe it might be boring over there with just Grandpa to talk to," he said.

"Yea, to tell you the truth, it is."

They both laughed.

"Would you like me to go over and visit you for awhile?" he asked.

"Sure, are your mom and brothers coming, too?" Willa asked.

"No, I'm the only one who will be going over. My mom is at work and my brothers are at day camp. I know how boring it is here at home and I have more to do than you do," he said.

"Let me ask Vesta first. I need to make sure it's all right with her," Willa said. "Hold on, I'll be right back," she added.

Willa put the receiver down and went to the living room where Vesta was sitting smoking a cigarette and watching TV.

"Vesta, Tony, your grandson, is who is on the phone and he wants to know if he could come over to visit for awhile today? I told him I would have to ask you first," Willa asked.

"Sure as long as the two of you don't make any noises and stay outside," she said.

Willa went back to the phone and told him, "She said it's okay for you to come over, we just can't make any noise and we have to stay outside in the back yard," Willa repeated what Vesta said.

"Okay, sounds good to me," he said. "I'll be down in about ten minutes. I have the car today," he said.

"Cool, you drive?" Willa asked.

"Yea, I've been driving since I turned sixteen," he said.

"Well, I have to get off the phone. They have me on a five-minute limit and I don't want to get into any trouble. I will see you when you get here," Willa told him and then hung up the phone.

Willa went back to the living room to play with her Barbie.

"What is the reason Tony wants to come over?" Vesta questioned.

"I guess he is bored at home, because Clara is at work and the other boys are at day camp," Willa answered.

"I find it kind of strange that a sixteen-year-old boy wants to come and visit a ten-year-old girl," Vesta said.

"I think he just wants to get to know me better. We just met and found that we are sort of cousins," Willa explained.

"Well, I hope that is his only intention. If anything goes wrong, you make sure to come tell me, do you hear?" Vesta demanded.

"Sure, I will," Willa said.

"What could go wrong?" Willa thought. "I guess Vesta doesn't trust him to be in the yard. I'll watch him closely. He won't mess anything up back there." Again she thought. Willa was also thinking how funny it would be to see Tony drive. It would look like Howdy Doody would be driving. She couldn't stop giggling as she colored in her book. Time went quickly because there was a knock at the front door and Vesta got up to answer it.

"It's Tony," she said.

"Wow, ten minutes goes by fast when you're not thinking about it," Willa thought.

"Hi, Tony," she said, glad to see him.

"Hi," he said back.

"The two of you go out back. I don't want to be disturbed while I'm watching my stories," Vesta told them.

"Come on, Tony, let's go to the back yard," Willa said.

She led the way and he followed. They got to the back yard and sat on the grass.

"What's up?" he asked.

"Nothing, I was just keeping myself busy, coloring in my books," Willa answered feeling embarrassed.

"What do you usually do for entertainment around here?" Tony asked her.

"I have my Barbie, paper dolls, and coloring books. That is mostly it. Sometimes Grandpa takes us somewhere like the zoo, museum, or another boring place," She told him, feeling her face getting red.

He laughed. Willa didn't think anything she had just told him was funny, but she laughed with him.

"What kind of music do you listen to?" Willa asked him.

"I like acid rock; I think that's the only kind of music that's cool," he responded.

They sat and talked a while longer.

"Willa," Vesta yelled. "You and Tony come in and wash up so you can eat some lunch," she said.

"Okay, we'll be right in," Willa said.

"Come on," Willa said as she got up from the ground. "Let's go in and eat lunch."

They both dusted themselves off while walking to the door to go in.

After lunch, they went out back again, talking about a lot of things. Willa told him about the neighbor staring out of his pantry window at her sometimes. Tony suggested she sit with her back to the house so he would be able to look at the window without the man knowing that he was looking right back at him. This way he could catch him staring out of the window. They both laughed, and sat in the position planned, but the man never looked out of his window.

"I guess he's not home today," Tony said. "Do you want to go for a ride?" he asked.

"Sure, I guess so, but first I have to ask Vesta if it's all right," Willa explained.

"Okay, I'll wait out here for you," he said.

Willa got up and went into the house to ask Vesta's permission. Vesta wasn't expecting Willa to come in. She was standing in the dining room drinking out of a bottle of whiskey.

"Oops, sorry, I didn't mean to intrude," Willa told her.

"Why are you sneaking around the house?" she yelled.

"I wasn't sneaking. I came in here to ask you if I could go for a ride with Tony in his car?" Willa asked reluctantly.

"No, absolutely not. You are my responsibility and if anything were to happen to you, I would be the one to get blamed. NO!" she shouted.

Willa turned and went back outside to let Tony know what Vesta said.

"I heard, she was yelling it loud enough for me to hear her all the way out here," he said.

"Oh, how embarrassing," Willa thought. Although Tony is Vesta's grandson, Willa still felt embarrassed that Vesta was yelling at her loud enough for the people outside to hear.

"She is in there drinking her whiskey. She's getting drunk and will be on the war path for awhile, because I caught her drinking," Willa explained.

"I know the feeling. My mom doesn't sneak to drink, but she gets pretty wild when she's been drinking whiskey," Tony told Willa.

"Come on, why don't you sneak out?" he asked. "When my mom is like that, I leave because I don't want to fight with her," he said.

"I can't sneak out, the gates are locked. I have already tried that once," she admitted.

"I better go. I don't want to be around to hear her. If she is anything like my mom, she will start yelling for stupid little thing," he said. "Before I leave, I want to ask you a question," he said.

Willa nodded in agreement.

"Do you have a boyfriend?" he asked.

Willa felt flushed all over. She felt the heat everywhere on her body.

"No, I don't," she responded.

"Would you like one?" he asked.

"I never thought of having one before," she lied. "I don't know? I guess I might," she said, feeling like her skin was burning up.

"I would like to be your boyfriend," he said.

Willa felt weird inside and could feel butterflies fluttering around all over the inside of her body.

"I don't know what to say," she said.

"Have you ever kissed a boy before?" he asked her.

"No, I've only kissed my brothers, Jason, my stepfather and my Grandpa," she admitted, thinking "Oh, how embarrassing. I am acting like a little girl, like a ten year old."

Tony leaned over and kissed her on the lips. Willa didn't know how to respond. The kiss felt good and his lips were so soft on hers. She kept her head down and couldn't look at him.

"What do I do now? Am I supposed to like it?" she thought.

"We can't be boyfriend and girlfriend," Willa told him.

"Why not?" he questioned.

"We are cousins, remember?" she reminded him.

"Only through the marriage of your Grandpa to my Grandma. We are not blood related," he explained.

Willa could still feel the butterflies fluttering around inside. They were good butterflies, not like the ones she gets when she is scared. She forgot all about his looks—that he looked like Howdy Doody.

"Okay, I'll be your girlfriend," she told him.

Then he leaned down to kiss her again.

"Get the fuck away from her, you pervert," Vesta yelled.

She was standing at the back door. They didn't know for how long, but she was furious.

"Get your fucking ass out of this yard, NOW," she yelled at him.

Tony got up and tried to get out of the gate, but it was locked.

"Go through the fucking house. I better not ever hear from you again."

She kept yelling at him and followed him out to the front porch making sure he left. Vesta turned around and Willa was standing in the living room.

"Didn't I tell you to come in and tell me if he tried anything?" she yelled.

"Yes," Willa whimpered; it was the only word she could utter.

"What else did he do to you?" she asked.

"Nothing, he only kissed me. He asked me if he could be my boyfriend," Willa explained, feeling like she was standing in front of Vesta stark naked.

Vesta lifted her hands to her forehead and shouted, "What the fuck is on that kid's mind? He knows you are only ten years old. He was sitting at the table when you told Clara how old you were," she blared.

Willa was shaking with fear; scared because of what she did. She didn't mean to do anything wrong, which was the wrong she did that felt so good for only a few minutes.

"He said it was okay because we were not related by blood," Willa tried to explain. "I didn't think it was wrong. I am so sorry, Vesta," she cried.

"Of course, you wouldn't. You are just a baby. You can't think straight when some smooth talking horny asshole is making you think it is okay," she said in a calmer voice. "Did he touch you anywhere?" she asked.

"No, he only kissed me," Willa told her.

"I don't know what to do. I can hardly wait until Sunday. Then your mom can have the responsibility back," she said. "We absolutely cannot tell your Grandpa any of this. He will hit the roof. There is no telling what he would do to you or me. There is no way I am going to tell him, and I don't want to get beaten for something you did," she said.

The rest of the afternoon seemed to take forever; Willa was coloring in her books while Vesta was off doing whatever she had to do. Willa couldn't stop thinking of the kiss, which made the situation in the house seem so much better.

Grandpa came home and both of them acted like nothing had happened. Everything went smooth; the same questions answered with the same answers. It was a typical day, at least that is what they wanted him to think. For the first time since she could remember, Willa was kind of glad that Grandpa had to go to work tomorrow, because he would have her sitting learning how to do the book work. He would ask her to give him specifics on the day she had. She didn't want to have to keep up the lies; it was hard enough keeping this secret from him this long. The secret of Clara and her children coming to visit was easy, because she was excited about meeting all of them and didn't want to stop seeing them. However, the secret she is keeping now is worse; this is something she did wrong. At bedtime, Willa found it hard to go to sleep. She kept thinking of how soft Tony's lips were on hers. She thought of how good it felt when he kissed her and the feeling she had inside. Then she remembered what he looked like. "Yuck," she thought. "I let Howdy Doody kiss me." She giggled softly, so no one could hear her. At the moment when Tony kissed her, and Vesta started yelling, it was very scary. Thinking about it now that it's over, it is a little funny. Vesta's words kept ringing in her ears, "Get away from her, you fucking pervert." Willa wanted to laugh out loud, but she didn't want to interrupt the quietness of the house. "I could tell my friends when I get back home, that I kissed a sixteen year old. I just won't tell them what he looks like. I could embellish that one," she thought, thinking her friends would think she was cool. Her thoughts of the day were reeling over and over until she finally fell asleep.

CHAPTER NINETEEN

It is Saturday, and Willa is glad it is finally here. This means she will get to go home tomorrow. Willa never thought she would miss home as much as she has, but she can hardly wait until she is again in her own room. Willa was in a deep sleep. She found it hard to wake up when Vesta shook her, telling her it was 7:45.

"What's wrong with you?" Vesta asked Willa.

"Nothing, why do you ask?" Willa was curious.

"I have been yelling at you for fifteen minutes and you wouldn't budge. Usually you wake up the first time I call your name." Vesta explained.

Willa couldn't think of what could be wrong. She didn't remember dreaming anything good or bad.

"I guess I am just more tired today," she explained.

"Well, go to the bathroom and splash some cold water on your face; that will wake you up," Vesta told her, and turned around and walked to her chair.

Willa got up and went to the bathroom. As she sat on the toilet, she felt herself drifting off to sleep again. Then she jumped when she heard banging on the door and Vesta yelling.

"Are you okay in there?" she yelled.

"Yes, I'm all right, Willa responded.

"You've been in there for ten minutes and I didn't hear the water running or any other noises. I just wanted to make sure you're all right," she hollered through the door sounding concerned. "Breakfast is almost ready. Hurry up and get out of there," she said.

Then Willa heard her footsteps as she went away. "Ten minutes?" she thought. "I must have fallen asleep on the toilet. It felt like I just closed my eyes."

She got up, dressed, washed her face, and combed her hair. Then she brushed her teeth. She hurried to do all of it so she wouldn't be late for breakfast.

Willa sat at the kitchen table.

"Tony tried calling for you this morning. I told him never to call here again," Vesta told her.

Willa sat quiet and didn't say a word; she thought it was all over. They both sat down to eat the omelets Vesta made. Willa doesn't like to eat eggs but she will eat them with lots of vegetables and meat in them. Willa couldn't help but to start thinking about Tony. "He called me, he must really like me. A sixteen-year-old boy likes me." She started thinking about the kiss at the breakfast table.

"Why are you just staring into your food?" Vesta asked.

"I don't know, I guess I'm still sleepy," Willa replied.

"Did that boy give you any drugs?" Vesta asked with a glare in her eyes.

"No, he didn't give me anything," Willa said.

"This is unusual, the way you are acting. You are usually wide awake at this time," Vesta said in an accusing voice.

"Honest, Vesta, he didn't give me anything, but two kisses, and that's all," Willa defended herself and Tony.

"You can't lie. I will find out the truth," Vesta said.

"Vesta, you've got to believe me. He didn't give me anything." Willa started crying.

"He may have slipped something into your mouth when you were kissing," she said.

"I don't think he did," Willa cried.

"Come to think of it, you were acting a little strange last night and I heard you giggle a couple of times when you were supposed to be trying to go to sleep," Vesta accused.

"I was laughing because I kept remembering how scared we were when you hollered at Tony. It wasn't funny then, but when I was relaxed and thinking about it, it made me giggle, because at that time is seemed funny to me," Willa admitted.

Willa didn't want to tell her she was laughing at her, but she needed to defend Tony from the accusations.

"I don't know," Vesta said. "I will find out one way or another, if you were on any drugs or not," she vowed.

They finished eating their breakfast and Vesta rose from her chair and asked, "Will you wash the dishes this morning? I need to get dressed and fix my bed."

"Sure, I will get them done," Willa promised.

Vesta went to her bedroom to do what she had to do and Willa stayed in the kitchen to wash the dishes. She cleaned the table and the stove, all along while thinking about Tony. She was thinking more about the kiss, than him. She could feel the good butterflies fluttering inside as she thought about that quick kiss. She was hoping that he would try to call again, or come and sneak to see her. Her thoughts were seeing him sneaking to the back gate while she was out back. Willa would go to Vesta and ask her permission to go to the store and she could meet Tony there. Willa thought hard about Tony, hoping he could hear or feel the thoughts, and they could get together again. Time passed quickly. Willa finished the dishes and was already putting them away, before she knew it. She didn't realize she was putting the dishes away until she walked out of the pantry. "Wow, I wonder if he did slip any drugs into my mouth yesterday?" she thought. Willa walked into the front room to fold the sheets and blankets, and to turn the bed into the sofa, since she hadn't done it before eating breakfast. "It's done! I guess Vesta came in here and fixed everything for me," she thought. Willa walked to the hallway and hollered into the closed door of the bedroom.

"Thank you, Vesta, for making the couch for me."

There was no response. "I guess she didn't hear me. I'll tell her when she comes out of her room," Willa thought.

Willa went to the back porch to the cleaning closet to get the vacuum cleaner. She bent down to pick it up when she heard a knock at the window, which startled her, because she wasn't expecting to hear anything. She looked up to see Tony's face staring in at her through the window. She ran to the porch screen door, and opened it. She went to the gate to talk to him.

"You better leave. Vesta might catch you here," she told him.

She was glad he came over to see her, but not now.

"I want to see you," he said. "For some reason, I can't get you out of my head," he told her.

"You can't stay right now. Meet me at Tom's store at about 9:30," Willa told him.

"Okay," he said. Then he turned around and left.

Willa went back inside to finish what she started. "I am so glad I didn't get caught by Vesta," she thought.

"Who were you talking to in the back?" Vesta asked.

"Oh, no! She saw us, and she knows," she thought.

"It was Tony. I told him he had to leave before we both get into trouble," Willa lied.

"I better not see that boy back here again or I will call the police," Vesta said.

Willa had no response. She looked down, turned on the vacuum cleaner, and started doing her chores. As she was cleaning the front room, she thought, "How could she be so cruel? That is her grandson. He didn't mean anything by kissing me," she thought. When she finished her vacuuming, she wrapped the cord neatly and went to put the vacuum cleaner back where it belongs. Willa kept looking at the clock to see what time it was, but since she stopped doing her chores, it seemed like the time was ticking by slowly. It seemed like it was an hour ago when it was 8:30, but it is only ten minutes later. Vesta was busy washing clothes today; she gathered all the sheets and blankets.

"I am glad Tony came when he did. I forgot that Vesta washes clothes on Saturday," she thought. Actually, she forgot all about today being Saturday.

"Willa, can you come here for a second?" Vesta called.

"Sure, here I come." Willa said.

She got up off the couch and went into the kitchen.

"I need you to go out and hang these blankets for me. My back is hurting and I don't want to lift anything heavy. Could you do that for me?" she asked.

"Yes," Willa said as she reached for the basket containing blankets from Vesta's hands.

Willa went outside to hang them, looking all around. She hoped Tony was somewhere she could see him, but she didn't see him anywhere. She went back into the house with the empty basket.

"Thank you for doing that for me. Those are the only two heavy items I have. I am not going to need you anymore," Vesta said.

"You're welcome. Vesta, at nine o'clock can I go to Tom's to get me some chips?" she asked.

"There are some in the pantry; you don't have to spend your money," Vesta said.

"Are they Fritos?" Willa asked. "Those are my favorite kind," she added.

"I don't think so, but you can go check and see. You know your Grandpa gets everybody their favorite brands of snacks," Vesta said.

Willa went into the pantry to look for the Fritos. "Shit," she thought. "There are Fritos in here." Willa grabbed the bag and brought it out to show Vesta.

"Yes, there are Fritos here." Willa showed her.

"See, you can hold onto your money for more important things," she said.

"What excuse am I going to use now?" she thought. Willa left the kitchen to go to the living room to see what time it was. She saw someone at the door peeking in. At first, she was scared because she didn't know who or what it was looking in at her. She thought of screaming for Vesta, but as she got closer she saw that it was Tony. "What's he doing here?" she thought. She turned to look at the clock and saw it was 9:45, fifteen minutes past the time she promised to meet Tony. Willa went to the screen door and opened it.

"It's already 9:45, what happened?" Tony asked in a concerned voice.

"I tried to make an excuse to go to the store and the only thing I could think of were chips," she explained.

Then she went on to tell him, "I told her I only wanted Fritos. She made me check in the pantry first before going to spend my money. Go sit under the front room window on the porch. I'll be out in a minute," she instructed him.

"Okay," he said, and went to sit down underneath the window.

Willa smiled, thinking she told him what to do and he did it. "He is sixteen, and he is a lot older than me." She felt proud of herself. She went into the kitchen to talk to Vesta.

"Vesta, promise not to get mad or call the police?" she asked.

"What's wrong?" Vesta gave her a side look.

"Tony is out front, and he wants to talk to me. I could find out from him if he slipped any drugs in my mouth yesterday. Nothing can happen sitting on the front porch and I promise not to go anywhere with him," Willa explained.

"Wow," she thought, "I am acting like I am sixteen now. I impressed myself in more ways than one today."

"Okay, I will trust you to make a good judgment. You have to stay where I could see you at all times. Do you hear me?" Vesta said.

"Yes, I hear you," Willa told her.

Willa turned and hurried through the house to go out to the front porch where Tony was waiting for her.

"Get up, you can sit on the couch. It's okay. Vesta knows you're here. I had to tell her because if she came and found you here, she would have called the police," Willa explained.

"Thank you," he said. "I miss you, ever since the first day we met; I can't stop thinking about you. I know you're only ten year's old."

"Soon to be eleven," Willa interrupted.

Somehow saying that she was almost eleven made her feel older than she was, and besides, ten sounds too young.

"Okay, soon to be eleven, but I can't get you out of my mind. Even more now since we kissed," Tony said, pouring his heart out to her. "Am I feeling this way alone? Or do you think about me too?" he asked her.

"I could hardly get to sleep last night thinking about you, thinking about us and what happened," Willa admitted.

He started to get close to her, because they were on opposite ends of the rattan couch.

"You have to keep your distance for now. I don't want you or me to get into any trouble. Vesta could be looking at us right now," Willa told him.

"Just hearing you talk to me makes me hard," Tony told her.

Willa looked at him with a puzzled look on her face.

"What does that mean?" she wondered.

"See, look," he said, pointing at his crotch area.

Willa looked down not knowing what she was going to see.

"Oh, my!" she said and turned her head feeling her face getting red.

"What's wrong? Haven't you ever seen a guy with a hard on?" he asked her.

Willa was too embarrassed to look at him again. She kept her head looking straight at the street.

"No, this is my first time," she told him.

"Well, what do you think?" he asked.

"I don't know. It's big. How did that happen?"

She was curious and besides those were the only words she could think of at that time.

"It happens every time I think of you, or see you, or hear your voice. It was difficult keeping it hidden the day we first met. I was hoping my mom or grandma wouldn't see it," he told her.

"I didn't know. Is it bad that I do that to you?" she asked him.

"No it isn't. As a matter of fact, it is good, because it means you excite me," he explained.

Willa didn't know what to think at that point, she was so confused.

"I want you. I don't want to hurt you," he said.

"I want you, too, I guess. To tell you the truth, this is all so embarrassing to me. I really don't know what to think," she told him.

"What about other girls your own age?" she questioned.

"What about them? I have girls who want me only because of sex, but I don't want them. I don't feel the same way about them as I feel about you. I can't stop thinking about you, and that is when this happens to me," he told her as he was rubbing himself.

Willa didn't know what to think. "What is going on here? Is it true what my mom says about me? Am I a temptress? Do I do this to all men and boys? Am I a whore? I don't want to be a whore." Thoughts were reeling through her mind.

"I really don't want to hurt your feelings, but I don't want to be a whore," Willa said.

"What? You are definitely not a whore. A whore is someone who sleeps with different men all of the time. You don't do that," he informed her.

"I don't know, this is all happening too fast, it's kind of scary," she told him. "I have heard about sex, but I have never seen anybody doing it and I have never done it," she told him.

"I don't expect sex from you," he said. "That would be considered child molesting or even statutory rape. I don't want to go to jail. I just want to be with you and to hold you every once in awhile. If I wanted sex, I could go to someone else to get it. Don't worry," he assured her.

Now she was really confused. "If he is supposed to be my boyfriend, why does he need to get sex from another girl? He shouldn't do it at all," she thought.

"I thought you asked me to be your girlfriend? If you want me to be your girlfriend, should you be going out to get sex with another girl?" she asked him.

"It gets boring to jack-off all the time. I need someone else to satisfy my lust," he explained.

If she wasn't confused by the things she had seen and heard before, she was even more confused by the words he was using now. She had never heard the words jack-off or lust, and she had no idea what those words meant. She was too embarrassed to admit that she didn't know.

"Couldn't you go without it?" she asked.

"I could try; it's just that once you've had it, it is kind of hard to stay away from it because it feels so good," he explained to her.

"Maybe we should get off this subject. He may think I am interested in doing it," she thought. She was feeling the good butterflies in her belly before, but now they were gone; fear and confusion was there. She didn't know what to think. Everything was going so fast, and besides, she is too young to think of things like that.

"What grade are you in?" she asked him, changing the subject.

"I am going into the tenth grade," he answered.

"Do you like high school?" she asked.

"It's all right; it's the same as being in any other school, only everyone is older now," he said.

"What do we talk about now?" she thought.

"Do you want some iced tea?" she asked him, breaking their silence.

She was feeling nervous, with him staring at her.

"Sure, I'll take a glass," he said.

Willa went into the house and to the kitchen where Vesta was still doing the laundry.

"I came in to get me and Tony a glass of iced tea," she told her.

"How is it going out there? Is he behaving himself?" Vesta asked.

"Yes, we are just talking about school and other things," Willa explained.

"It's almost time for lunch. Go ask him if he will give us a ride to McDonald's to get something to eat," Vesta said.

"Okay, I will go now instead of serving the tea," Willa said.

Then she hurried through the house to ask him, but when she got out to the porch, he was gone. "Where did he go?" she thought, as she looked around the house and out on the street. There was no sign of him and no sign of his car. She went back into the house to let Vesta know he had left.

"He left. He was gone when I went back out to the porch," Willa said.

"It's okay, you and I could go walking. It is only about five blocks away. Do you want to walk with me?" Vesta asked.

"Yeah, I'll go with you," Willa said.

Vesta changed into her shoes from her slippers and they went to go get their lunch.

That night, Willa had another one of her nightmares. There is a man sitting in the pantry. He is calling her to him, and telling her (without moving his lips), "It's okay, don't worry, I'll take care of you."

"I don't know him, do I?" she thought. Is it grandpa?

"Is that you, grandpa?" she cries.

She cannot see his face. There is a bright light glowing inside the pantry window making it hard to see anything but a big dark shadow.

She slowly moves toward him hoping he is her grandpa. Then he will help her get away from those things trying to grab at her from the cellar, and the rats and mice that are crawling around at her feet. She gets close enough to look at him. He has no face and there are only two glowing red dots where his eyes should be. She tries to scream but she can't. It feels as though she lost her voice. He is calling her name.

"Willa, come to me. I will take care of you. Willa, I can help you. Come look into my eyes. You can trust me," he assures her.

He wants her to look into his eyes. What eyes? Why? There are only two red glowing dots where his eyes should be. At this point, she doesn't care who he is or what he wants. She only wants to get out of the house. She woke herself up because she found it hard to breathe. She wouldn't let the dream go all the way and she tried to think of more pleasant things to dream about. The pleasant thoughts were only around while she was awake. However, when she fell back to sleep, she was haunted by that same nightmare. A man is sitting in the pantry.

He is calling her to him, telling her (without moving his lips), "It's okay. Don't worry, I'll take care of you."

"I don't know him, do I?" she thought. Is it grandpa?

"Is that you, grandpa?" she cries.

She cannot see his face. There is a bright light glowing inside the pantry window making it hard to see anything but a big dark shadow. She slowly moves toward him hoping he is her grandpa. He will help her get away from those things trying to grab at her from the cellar, and the rats and mice that are crawling around at her feet. She gets close enough to look at him. He has no face and there are only two glowing red dots where his eyes should be. She tries to scream but she can't. It feels as though she's lost her voice. He is calling her name.

"Willa, come to me. I will take care of you. Willa, I can help you. Come look into my eyes. You can trust me," he assures her.

He wants her to look into his eyes. What eyes? Why? There are only two red glowing dots where his eyes should be. At this point, she doesn't care who he is or what he wants. She only wants to get out of the house. Again, she woke up. She couldn't get that nightmare out of her head, but she couldn't stay awake because there was too much time until it would reach morning or at least until the first light. "I wish I was at home. I wish I could be a baby again. I don't remember when I was a baby, so that had to be the best time of my life," she thought. "Maybe, I'm having these nightmares because I kissed Tony. Maybe because the way Tony and I were talking to one another on the porch earlier today, that could be one way of having sex. Maybe it is because I looked at his crotch area. I didn't see anything really—only a big bulge in his pants, and him rubbing on it. Maybe I shouldn't have looked at that. Maybe I am a whore like mom said I was? Maybe because I didn't tell Grandpa the entire truth about Clara and her boys visiting Vesta when he was at work, and Tony's extra trips to visit her personally. Maybe this is God's way of punishing me?" So many thoughts were reeling in her head. She didn't want to dream anymore because it made her so scared that she would lose her breathe.

"Dear Lord," Willa prayed, "please forgive all of my ugly thoughts. Please forgive me for looking at things I'm not supposed to look at. Please forgive me all of my lies, and the secrets that I've been keeping. Please forgive me for everything. Please help me to go to sleep and not dream. Now I lay me down to sleep. I pray the Lord my soul to keep. If I should die before I wake, I pray the Lord my soul to take."

Before she knew it, she fell asleep and this time without having a nightmare.

Chapter Twenty

Willa's eleventh year went pretty good. She spent a lot of time at summer day camp and she met a lot of new friends there. She really didn't have time for any bad dreams; she never even thought of them. She was having too much fun doing all the fun things an eleven-year-old girl would enjoy. She learned archery, and how to sew, plus she went swimming just about every other day. There were a couple of times when the camp would have a dance and the girls and boys had to dance with each other. The girls had some alone time so Willa decided to tell her new friends about Tony. She told them how they had kissed and gotten caught by Vesta, and the time on the front porch. They all giggled when she got to the part of looking at his crotch area. Everyone was curious to know what it looked like.

"I've only seen it through his pants. The pants were covering it up," she explained. "I didn't see the real thing. I was too afraid to look at the pants. Could you imagine if I saw the real thing? I probably would have fainted," she giggled with them.

That was the favorite story of the group Willa was in. She figured why not talk about everything that happened. She couldn't keep it in forever and besides she probably would never see Tony again since she wasn't staying at Grandpa's house during the weekdays this summer. Anyway, that is when Clara and the boys went to visit Vesta. None of the other girls could top Willa's story. She was proud because she was somewhat popular. It didn't matter to her why or how she got her popularity—she only wanted to fit in somewhere and here she did fit in with the girls in her group. Even though she had to go home every afternoon, she knew she was going to go to day camp the next day, which made her happy.

One afternoon when she went home, Esther quizzed her, "Guess who is coming over for dinner tonight?" she asked.

"I don't know? Who is?" Willa asked curiously excited.

"Clara and her three sons. We've been keeping in touch with each other since that time you gave me her phone number," Esther said.

Willa turned white, like she had seen a ghost. She could feel all of the blood draining from her face.

"What's wrong?" Esther asked. "Is there something wrong with you, Willa?" she asked again.

"No, nothing is wrong. I guess I shouldn't have gone running after eating lunch today. We were all hyper and went out to play kick ball," Willa lied.

"Well, go upstairs and get cleaned up. I want you to look good for tonight. I don't want them to think you look this way all the time," Esther told her. "While you're up there, you should get some rest. You look pale. You need to get some color back into your face," she added.

"I don't want to be here tonight. I wish Grandpa would come and get me now," she thought.

"What about Grandpa? Isn't he coming over to get me today?" Willa asked.

"No, I called him up and let him know you wouldn't be going over this weekend, because I have another surprise. Jacob rented a cabin in the mountains for the weekend and I have invited Clara and her boys to stay with us," she said excitedly.

Willa felt like Esther had gotten a knife and plunged it into her chest, and the more Esther talked, the further the knife went in. Everything went quiet. Esther was still talking but Willa could no longer hear the words. Her head started to spin, and she had to run upstairs to throw up.

"I don't want to see Tony. I told my friends about him and we all laughed at him. What if he starts talking to me like he did on the porch, again? What if he tries to kiss me and someone sees us? Mainly my mom, she would for sure hate me."

More worrisome thoughts were spinning around in her head.

Willa went into her room to lie down and before she knew it, Esther was waking her up.

"Our company is here," she said. "I want you to get dressed and then come downstairs," Esther ordered.

Willa got up and looked for something to wear. She went to the bathroom and got dressed, combed her hair and washed her face. She didn't want to see anybody; she felt like crying and could feel a large lump in her throat. Willa walked down the stairs. Her head started spinning and the bad feelings of butterflies were fluttering around in her stomach. "What am I going to say? How am I going to act? I have to calm down," she thought. Willa reached the bottom step, took a few deep breaths, and then walked into the living room.

"Hi, Willa," Clara said.

"Hi," Willa responded.

"Did you just wake up?" Clara asked.

"Yeah, I think I might have gotten sun stroke from being out in the sun too long today," she told her.

Willa remembered hearing Esther say to someone once when Serge was sick from being out in the sun all day, that he came in tired, then started throwing up, and then he fell asleep for the rest of the day—so that is why she told the story to Clara. Willa looked around but saw only Clara.

"Where are your boys?" Willa asked.

"The two younger ones are out in the back yard with your brothers, and Tony went with Jacob to order a couple of folding beds, some cots, or something," Clara explained.

Willa was really hoping to hear, "The two younger boys are out in the back yard with your brothers and Tony couldn't make it, he had something else to do this weekend." Those were the words she wanted to hear, but somehow she knew she had to see Tony.

"Willa, could you come in here?" Esther called.

"Sorry," Willa apologized to Clara. "I don't want to be rude, but my mom is calling for me," she said.

"It's okay, go ahead and go, I'll be fine." Clara assured her.

Willa went to the kitchen where her mom was waiting.

"Yes," she said.

"I need you to set the dining room table for the adults and then come back in here and set the table for the kids," Esther said.

"Could I eat in the dining room with you?" Willa asked.

"No, why do you ask?" Esther was curious.

"I don't feel good," Willa explained, thinking that is definitely not a lie because her stomach was churning.

"Oh, and you want to get sick all over us?" Esther questioned sarcastically.

"No, I just don't want to be with a bunch of rowdy boys. They will be jumping around making me sicker," Willa explained.

"I don't think that is going to happen," Esther said. "Oh, by the way, set a plate in the dining room for Tony. He is too old to be eating with you kids," Esther told her.

"Okay, I will," Willa responded.

"What did I almost do?" she thought. "I almost had to sit at the same table where he would be. I am glad he is older—that way he doesn't have to sit with us. I guess God really is looking out after me," she thought. Willa gathered the dishes and the silverware, and went into the dining room to set the table. As she was finishing up, Jacob and Tony walked in the front door. Willa tried to keep her head down; she didn't want to look up. She felt like she had done something wrong and was hoping she didn't look guilty. "Not now, I don't want mom to embarrass me in front of everybody," she thought. She straightened herself up and went into the kitchen to set the table in there. As she was gathering the dishes and the silverware, Esther announced that she was going to go to the living room to talk with everyone. Willa was in the kitchen all by herself, when Tony came in to talk to her.

"Hi, how are you?" Tony asked.

"Fine, how are you?" Willa responded, not wanting to look nervous.

"I'm doing pretty good," he said. "I was a little shocked when your mom invited my family to go for the weekend with your family to the mountains," he said.

"Oh? Why?" Willa asked, still keeping her head down as to look as if she was concentrating on the order of the table.

"Because of what happened between the two of us," he said. "I thought for sure someone would be wanting to kill me. At first, I was afraid to go, but my mom talked me into it. She said that if I didn't go, I could start looking for another place to live. I figured the reason for them inviting me is so that they could kill me in the mountains," he explained.

"Well, don't worry, I never told anyone about what happened. Vesta and I kept it our little secret, and I never told anyone—not even Vesta—anything about what happened on the porch," she told him.

"It's been a long time since we've seen each other. I am really glad I have this chance to see you again. I want to apologize for anything I said or done at that time. I should have known better than to do or say any of those things," he said.

"It's okay, what's done is done. There is nothing any of us can do to change the things that have happened in our past. We can just live for what is to come," Willa told him.

"Wow! Where did those words of wisdom come from? I know I said them, but I couldn't believe they were coming out of my mouth," she thought.

"Thanks, I needed to hear those words of encouragement from you. There is just one thing I need to get off my chest before I go back into the living room. I really did love you then and I thought I could get over you, but I couldn't. I figured that if I did come over to see you again, I would see how young you really are, and get over this feeling that I have been carrying. To tell you the truth, I still love you. I have never felt this way about anyone in my whole life. The sad thing is I can't have you, because you are too young. I was hoping that when you get old enough, we could see each other, like going out on a date or something—that you will want to see me. I am hoping that you won't have a boyfriend at that time and don't want to have anything to do with me," he said.

Then he turned around and left before Willa had a chance to say anything to him. He went back into the living room. Willa was able to get a good look at the person who used to remind her of Howdy Doody. He had grown up since then in only a year. He now was very muscular, his hair was still red and he still had freckles, but his body is nice. "I wish I could have told him, 'I will wait for you when I grow up. I don't want any other boyfriends besides you." She thought about it, and was glad she didn't get the chance to tell him, because she didn't know if she was feeling the way she was feeling because she really does love him, or because she learned what the word lust meant. Was it that she was just lusting for him, or was she feeling that way because she felt sorry for him because of what he just said about being in love with her? Her emotions were going crazy; she didn't know what to think.

Esther came into the kitchen to check on the food.

"Good, we can eat now," she said. "The food is all done and the tables are set; it's time to eat. Willa, call the boys in to come wash up for supper," she said.

Esther never asked anyone to do anything. She demanded they do whatever she said.

"Okay," Willa said, and then went to the back yard and called the boys in.

She informed them that they had to go wash up before they could sit down and eat. During supper, Willa couldn't get Tony's words out of her thoughts—the ones that he said that he still loves her. Again, those wonderful butterflies had entered her entire body and she felt good again. After dinner, the younger boys had to go get into their pajamas so they could settle down for the night. Esther, Clara and Willa cleaned up the tables and washed, dried and put away the dishes. Jacob and Tony packed the trunks of the cars so everything would be ready when they would all leave at five o'clock in the morning to start on their trip to the mountains.

The next morning, Esther was waking everybody up, saying, "Get up and get dressed. It's four o'clock."

Willa could hear the boys running through the hallway to get to the bathroom, so she decided to get dressed in her own room. When she went downstairs, she glanced over at Tony and he was staring at her. She was hoping that Esther or any of the others didn't see that. Everyone ate breakfast. Then, while the women were doing the dishes, the boys were getting situated in the cars. All the boys rode with Tony and Clara, and Willa rode with Jacob and Esther. Everything went good that weekend. The men went fishing while the women got situated the first day, and the evening came and went. There were no confrontations and not one bad thing happened. Esther didn't accuse Willa of trying to seduce all of the guys. Willa felt like a regular person, and she was actually having fun with her family for the first time in her life. "Who would have thought that things could look so good? Certainly not me," she thought. The trip went smoothly, and everyone wore their best faces, especially Esther. She was acting like she actually liked Willa and cared about her. Although this has been Willa's wish for as long as she can remember, she was getting a little irritated of getting that much attention from her mom. Another complaint Willa had about that weekend was that Tony stayed as far away from her as he possibly could. Willa didn't think anyone would have suspected anything was going on between the two of them if they just talked. She needed to ask him, "What happened the last day we saw one another? I went into the house and when I came back out to the porch, you were gone. Why did you leave? Was it something I said or did?" She never got to ask, and she figured maybe it was better that she never knew.

Willa's twelfth birthday is next weekend and she is going to be spending it at Grandpa's house. Although they do things for her, like taking her out to eat and to the mall to buy her whatever she wants, it's just not the same as having a birthday party with all her friends there. But she figured she shouldn't complain. She is so excited that she is almost in her teen years, and is going to start junior high school after summer break. She felt like she is getting old—old enough to date Tony. "Does he know I am going to be twelve soon? Will I see him again after this weekend is over?" she thought, starting to feel the emptiness of missing him again.

Chapter Twenty-one

The weekend is here. Today is Friday and Grandpa will be coming for the ritual weekend visit. Willa packed her clothes and got ready to go before Grandpa got there, because he gets impatient and does not like to wait around. Willa starts to remember when she was younger and had to pack her bags according to how Esther wanted her to dress. "You're a girl, Willa, and you need to act like one, no matter how hard it is," Esther would tell her. Willa always wanted to dress in jeans, just like her brothers. Now she has her own jeans and can wear them anytime she wants to. The only exceptions are when she goes to church on Sundays and when she goes to school. Now besides being able to pack jeans in her bag, she has to pack maxi pads because she started her menstrual cycle last month. Willa was surprised when it happened. The day camp that she was attending had evening tickets to the Central City Opera, which is in Central City, Colorado. So everyone from the day camp went to the opera that evening. Willa was feeling uncomfortable all evening. At the end of the program, she had to go to the restroom because she was drinking lots of pop. She was feeling thirstier than ever. When she went to the bathroom and afterward she wiped, it felt sort of slimy, but she didn't think anything of it. When she got home and had to go to the bathroom again, that is when she freaked out. Willa saw the blood on her panties and screamed for Esther. Esther came running to see what was going on.

"What's wrong?" Esther asked her.

"I don't know, look," Willa told her showing Esther her panties that were stained with blood. "I didn't do anything. I was just sitting in my seat the entire length of the show. Honestly, I didn't do anything wrong," Willa cried.

Esther said, "That is the sign that you are now coming into womanhood. It's called a menstruation period. You will get them every month from now on and they last about a week. You had better watch out for the boys now. They can smell you when you are having your menstruation period and they will all come after you for sexual favors. The dogs will start sniffing your butt, and they will try to goose you, too," she told her.

Willa was actually afraid to have another period. What if there is a boy around and she is on her period? What will he do to her? She was so glad that Ruby was no longer living next door to Grandpa because her dogs would probably attack her when she went out to sit in the back yard. She could just see it now. She would be relaxing, and writing on her book, and the dogs would jump over the fence and attack her. "I'll be too dead to know what happened. What if I didn't die and have to suffer from the attack all of my life?" she thought. "I have to get all this out of my mind and pay attention to getting my bag packed before Grandpa gets here," she thought as she finished packing for the weekend.

Willa was excited because she was going to go to the mall tomorrow and pick out whatever she wanted. The only bad thing about it was she would have to wait until Grandpa got home from work, and finished his shopping errands. Tomorrow is the Saturday he has to go to work. Willa remembered to pack her little binders to take with her so she could document everything about her weekend, making sure there were plenty of papers in them so she won't be running out. She looked at the bag before closing it and saw that she had packed enough stuff to go on a trip for a month. Willa took the binders filled with lots of paper so she could write all of her thoughts. She likes boys more these days, and they look a lot different to her. She can remember when she wouldn't give them a second look, but now they seem to be getting cuter. The boys are mainly why she writes. These binders are a throw-away diary to her because after she is finished writing about a boy that she likes, she tears up the page and then throws it away. Esther never bought her a diary because she said, "A diary is a tool for girls to do all the bad things they want and it's okay, because writing about it in their diary makes it all better and they can clear their conscience. Absolutely not—you cannot have one," she told Willa. Willa wondered if Grandma Emma was a Neanderthal because of the way her mom thought—it was so far back in time, it was pathetic. Esther's ideas, her ways, and her thoughts were thought to have something to do with evil. Nothing was ever good to her. Willa would sometimes wonder how Esther made it this far in life with her beliefs. Again, trying to make sure she had everything packed, she made sure to take a couple of books to read, because it gets boring at Grandpa's. She is much too old to play with those old boring paper dolls. Now that she is going to be twelve tomorrow and will be starting junior high school in the fall, she has to make sure she acts more mature—more like a grown-up—no more little girl things in her life anymore. At least this summer has been a lot more fun than any other summer that she could remember. Mostly she either wrote about something during the summer or winter. She wrote about the nightmares she had experienced—the most horrible experiences—whether she was awake or when she was sleeping. "It's not going to happen anymore. It hasn't happened in a long time and I refuse to let anything bad happen to me ever again. I am having the time of my life. I am a complete person with no more fears. I met new friends this year and I have had new experiences. I can do it. I am going to be a completely different person from now on. When I get to Grandpa's house, I will confront my personal demons. I will look at Grandma Emma's picture and the elk head, and know in my heart that they are inanimate objects. They cannot hurt me. The only thing that can get in my way now is my imagination, and I have control over it now. These were just some of the things she made promises to herself in her throw-away diary.

Willa heard Grandpa downstairs talking to Esther. She didn't want to keep him waiting because she knew for a fact that he didn't like being in their house for too long. Willa grabbed her suitcase and went downstairs.

"Good-bye, Willa," Serge yells from his bedroom. "Have a fun weekend, and have a happy birthday," he added.

"Thanks Serge, I will," Willa responded.

"Oh, yeah," she heard Ron say. "Happy birthday," he said.

"Thanks Ron," Willa said.

She went downstairs to say good-bye to her mom. Jacob wasn't home yet.

"Bye, Mom. I'll see you Sunday night," Willa told her.

"Bye, happy birthday. We will go to your Grandpa's tomorrow to take you your birthday present," Esther said.

"Sounds good. I will see everybody tomorrow then," Willa responded.

"Are you ready to go?" Grandpa asked.

"Yes, let's get out of here," Willa said.

They left the house and got into the car. They both put their seat belts on.

"I have to stop by the store on our way to the house," Grandpa told her.

"Okay," Willa said.

"How was your trip to the mountains last weekend?" Grandpa asked, sounding a little irritated at that question.

It made Willa feel a little uneasy.

"It went really well. Jacob and the boys all went fishing while mom, Clara and I cleaned up the cabin and collected twigs of wood to burn in the fireplace," she told him.

Willa thought that is what he wanted to hear. It was the truth, and she didn't lie about anything.

"Willa, I have something on my mind. Vesta told me something that had happened at our house sometime last year. I want you to tell me the truth," he said. "You owe me that much," he added.

Willa started to get scared. "Oh, God, what did Vesta tell him, to make him sound so irritated at me?" Willa knew for a fact that Grandpa was angry. He always calls her Princess and this time he called her by her name.

He went on, "Vesta told me that her grandson, Tony, went to the house and she caught the two of you kissing in the back yard. Is that true?"

He was getting red. Willa could see a vein in his temple throbbing.

"Yes, it's true; I didn't know at the time that I shouldn't be doing that. I didn't know it was a bad thing to do. I'm sorry," Willa cried.

"I am not entirely mad at you. I am more disappointed in you. Why didn't you come to me and tell me what happened?" he asked her in an angry manner.

Willa could see the disappointment in his face and she heard it in his voice. It made her feel like the lowest of the lowly.

"I was afraid, when I saw how mad Vesta was. I knew you would be equally or more mad at me. I don't mind too much when Vesta is angry with me because she is always mad at me for some reason. I just couldn't stand it if you were to be mad at me. When Vesta saw how scared I was, she said we would keep it our secret as long as I promised to never do it again. I promised her I wouldn't and I didn't do it ever again," she cried.

"Did he try anything with you besides kissing? I know you told Vesta that he didn't, but Princess, I need to be sure,"

Willa could see the tears welling up in his eyes.

"No, Grandpa, I swear to God, he didn't do or try anything else that day. Vesta came out just when he kissed me so it wasn't a long kiss," she sobbed.

"What about in the mountains?" he asked. "Did he try anything with you then?" he questioned, wanting to hear the truth.

"No, he was keeping busy with Jacob and the boys. I was close to mom and Clara most of the time," she explained.

"I believe you, Princess, but what I need you to do is promise me that if anything like that should ever happen again, you will tell me about it. Don't keep it a secret from me, no matter what anyone says. I need you to give me your word on that, because I know you won't go back on your word," he said wanting assurance.

"I promise, I don't think that will ever happen again. Vesta told him she would call the police if he comes to the house again," Willa told him.

"I know, she told me. There are other boys out there, Princess. They are ready to pounce on pretty girls like yourself," he said in a concerned voice. "You are a pre-teen now and you are a lot prettier now. I just want you to be safe; I promise you that if you ever get hurt by anyone, I will personally take care of that person. You have my promise on that and my word is as good as gold. I love you with all my heart, and when I heard about that incident, the only thing on my mind was to go find and kill that kid," he said.

"I love you, too, Grandpa," she said knowing that he meant every word he told her.

When they got to the store, the conversation stopped. Grandpa parked the car and shut the engine off.

"I don't feel like going in, right now, Grandpa. My eyes and nose are red from crying and I don't want to be stared at," Willa told him.

"No problem; is there anything special you want me to get for you?" he asked.

"Get some Coke; we never get to drink soda," Willa said, thinking she had to give him some kind of answer, because she didn't want him to think that she was angry at him.

"Okay, but what about your complexion? Won't the cola give you pimples?" he asked.

Then before she could say a word, he added, "Oh, well, as long as you are not worried about it, I won't be either. Is that it?" he asked.

Willa shook her head, and said, "That's all I can think of right now."

Before shutting the door, he asked her, "Are you sure you don't want to come in? You might find something that you want."

"I'm sure, I just want to stay here, but thanks for asking," she responded.

He shut the door and walked into the store. "Why would Vesta tell him our secret? How could she betray the trust I had in her?" Willa could not believe that Vesta is more vindictive than she could ever have imagined her to be. Knowing she would have gotten into trouble herself for keeping it from him for so long, Willa couldn't understand why Vesta decided to tell him now? Willa figured that because she and Tony were going to be in the mountains together for the weekend, anything could happen there. "I appreciate the concern she has, but I wish I was more prepared for what just happened," she thought. At this point, Willa was so grateful that the trip went the way it did, and that Tony had kept his distance from her. Willa was also grateful for Grandpa keeping his cool, because she was terrified that she was going to get hit, as mad as Grandpa looked. She thought for sure he was going to do something. As thoughts kept coming into her head, fear struck again, "Does my mom know about this? Oh, God, please let the answer be no. She hasn't said anything to me. Maybe that is the reason why she kept me close to her while we were there. No, I think she was keeping me close because the trip was planned and they all kept to the order of things. Also she was paranoid about my starting my period, and she absolutely wanted to keep me from being around any boys." Thoughts kept coming and they didn't seem to stop. Willa was getting desperate now. She needed to know if her mom knew anything about the kiss—that way she could be better prepared when Esther hits her with it and starts accusing her of doing things. "Why can't my life be calm for a complete year? Why must something happen to destroy the fun? I know one thing for sure. I will never allow myself to ever get caught in a predicament again. I am going to stay alone; I am the only person I can trust in this world. I must have known that from the beginning. I just couldn't see the complete picture. I have to remember to stop looking at the world through rose-colored glasses. From now on, it is going to be me against everyone and everything. That I promise to myself."

Grandpa came back to the car and put the groceries into the trunk.

"Sorry I took so long in there. It seems like everyone in this town had the same idea to come to the same store as I did," he said with a laugh.

They laughed together. The drive to Grandpa's house was quiet and neither of them said a word. Vesta was waiting at the door as usual when they drove up. Willa got out of the car, grabbed her bag out of the trunk, and walked up to the porch.

"Hi, Willa, how was your trip to the mountains?" Vesta asked.

"That is the first question she had to ask?" Willa thought, feeling hate toward her.

"It was okay; we had a lot of fun. Thank you for asking Vesta," Willa said with a smile.

Then Willa got a look at Vesta's face. She had a bruise on her cheek. She wanted to cry for thinking bad of her. Willa wanted to tell her, "I am sorry, I never meant to cause you any pain." But she couldn't get those words out especially since Grandpa was right there.

"How are you doing, Vesta?" Willa asked, making sure everything would seem normal.

"I'm doing fine. Thanks for asking," Vesta responded.

Willa reached around her and gave her a hug.

"I love you, Vesta," Willa told her.

Vesta looked at her with surprise.

"I love you, too. What brought that on?" she asked in shock.

"I really do love you, nothing more, nothing less," Willa told her.

They all went into the house. Willa had to get all of her stuff put away. Grandpa and Vesta had to go into the kitchen to put away the groceries, giving everyone something to do. It was only 4:00 p.m. when everyone finished doing what they had to do, so they congregated into the living room to watch TV, sew, and write.

"I have a suggestion," Vesta said interrupting the silence between them.

She was looking both at Grandpa and Willa.

"Carl, every year you take the Princess here out to eat for her birthday," she said, looking at Grandpa. "We all know that you are going to take us out tomorrow. I want to give her something from only me this year. I want to treat us out to supper tonight, and then we can go to the mall and let her pick something out from me. Tomorrow can be your day to do that for her, but I feel that I need to have a day for her from me," she said, still looking at Grandpa.

There was silence. Everyone was looking at one another.

"What do you say?" she asked him.

"I think that is a great idea. How about you, Princess? What do you think about that?" he asked Willa.

"It sounds like a lot of fun, and I say yes, let's do that," Willa said to both of them.

"I want to take you somewhere special tonight. Well, what I mean is I want you to choose where we go to eat," Vesta told her.

"I really don't know any restaurants; I haven't had the opportunity to go to very many," Willa told them.

"It's okay; I am leaving that decision up to you. You are going to be twelve tomorrow and now is as good a time as any to start making your own decisions," Vesta told her, as she turned to Grandpa and said, "Don't you think that's fair Carl?"

"Yes, I think you are correct. Listen to her, Princess. She knows what she is talking about. You need to learn about decision-making now so you can be prepared in adulthood," he told Willa.

"Okay then, how about that Chinese restaurant we go to get the take-out food? Can we eat there instead of bringing it home?" she asked.

"Are you sure you want to go there?" Vesta asked.

Willa didn't know what to think. "What is this? Is it a trick question? Was that the wrong answer?" she thought. "Was there something wrong with the answer?"

"Yes, I like their food and I know how the food tastes. I want to go there," Willa assured them.

"Fine, that is where we are going to eat our supper tonight," she said.

After all was said and done, Willa thought, "Whoa, I didn't know how to answer that one." She didn't know what they were expecting from her. It was not that she was complaining, because she liked being the center of attention as well as the next person, but this was all just a little too much, too fast for her. She doesn't mind change but this is drastic. "I hope this change in Vesta isn't because Grandpa threatened her to be nice to me. I couldn't take it if that were the case. I want Vesta and I to have the closeness because she wants it, and not because she is forced into it. Because for sure she will hate me even more," she thought, and the more she thought about it, the more Willa could see that the suggestion seemed somewhat staged, like Vesta was reading from some cue cards.

Grandpa announced that they all better be leaving now if they were going to have enough time to eat and then go to the mall, since it closes at 7:00 p.m. They all left to go to the restaurant and ordered their food. Grandpa and Vesta were talking and Willa was quietly waiting for the food to come. When the waitress brought the food, they ate, and talked about Willa's week at home. Grandpa and Vesta asked her if she knew what she was getting from her mom for her birthday. Everything seemed to be going perfectly. "I don't like this; it seems to plastic. I am not going to complain—no way, because it will just mess up a perfect evening," she thought. Willa is a slow eater, so Grandpa and Vesta were done before she was, which gave them time to smoke their cigar and cigarette. Grandpa didn't allow smoking in his car, so they had to fill their lungs with smoke in the restaurant. They finished smoking before Willa was finished eating. So she asked, "I'm full, do you think I could take this home and I could have it for lunch tomorrow?"

"Sure," Grandpa said. "Waitress," he called.

She came over, and he asked, "Could you please put this in a doggie bag for us?"

"Sure," she said, picking up the plate and leaving the check on the table.

Vesta picked up the check and went to pay for supper. When the waitress brought the box containing the food, they all got up to leave for the mall. Willa knew what she wanted since her favorite color is purple. The first store they went into Willa found the dress she wanted. It was mainly purple with some black, and then they went to the shoe department in the store. She got some patent leather shoes to match. They didn't stay at the mall as long as they stayed at the restaurant, and Grandpa was happy that Willa was able to make up her mind so quickly. As soon as Vesta paid for the clothes and shoes, they all left and went out to the car. They all headed for the house. Everyone was tired and they wanted to get back home as soon as possible. When they got inside, Willa gave Vesta a big hug.

"Thank you for supper and for the dress and shoes, Vesta," she said.

Then the night went back to its regular schedule. Grandpa and Vesta watched TV and smoked, while Willa wrote in her pages. At the appropriate time, they all went to bed, making sure the schedule was not interrupted.

CHAPTER TWENTY-TWO

It is Saturday morning and Grandpa has already left for work.

"I'm twelve years old today!" Willa said, excited.

She got up and did her regular morning routine. She could smell bacon cooking and it smelled good. The front door was open and she could hear the birds chirping. "I am so glad that today I am finally twelve." Vesta is busy in the kitchen cooking and Willa is in the bathroom getting cleaned up and dressed. She gets finished, then goes to fold the sheets and blankets and fold the bed back into a couch—all before Vesta had a chance to call her to go eat.

She went into the kitchen and announced, "I'm finished already. I just thought I would let you know," Willa told Vesta, and then she turned around and walked back to the living room.

"Willa, come in here," Vesta demanded.

"Oh, what's wrong now? Is she mad because I went into the kitchen?" Willa knew she was in some sort of trouble just listening to the sound of Vesta's voice. She hurried back to see what trouble she was in.

"Yes," she said.

"I know today is your birthday and you are going to get lots of surprises. Well, there is one surprise I have to tell you, and it is something you may or may not like. Your mom called your Grandpa early this morning and she was very upset. She does not know if she will be able to make it over here today. The reason being, is Jacob left your mom last night!"

Willa couldn't believe what she just heard. "I don't want to hear anymore. Stop!" she thought. But she had to stand there and listen to Vesta ramble on and on about it. Willa thought, "I sure could use my closet at this time, to sit and think about everything that is going on, and to disappear from everyone and everything. I really need to be alone," she thought. Jacob is the one person who would comfort Willa when her mom was being mean and accusing her of doing ugly things. Willa asked Vesta if she could go back to the living room and sit alone for a while. Vesta allowed her to go. She slowly walked through the dining room, then the long dark hallway, then into the living room, and then to the front room to get her folders and pencils. Then she went back to the living room and sat down to write. "Without Jacob, I don't want to ever go back to that house again. I wonder how the boys are taking it. I hope Mom isn't taking this out on them. It's not their fault; it is her fault for being such a bitch. Sometimes I just want to kill her. This is one of the times." After Willa wrote these words on the paper, she tore the paper into several pieces and then threw them away. Her thoughts were reeling, "What is she going to do now? She has never worked and she has no talent to do anything but bitch. I don't think anyone would hire her for that," she giggled silently. "Tony, where are you now? I'll have sex with you now. I may as well; I know my life is going to be more miserable from now on and because I am always accused of being a whore, why not be one?" she thought. "Well, happy birthday to me." She went on feeling sorry for herself. "This day has not started out good. I don't want my birthday anymore. Just make it go away."

While she was wallowing in self-pity, Vesta called out to her, "Willa, it's time to eat," she said.

Willa went into the kitchen with her eyes blurry with tears. She didn't think she could eat as upset as she was, but if she didn't eat, she would get into lots of trouble from Vesta, since she went to all the trouble of cooking. "I can't win. I wish today was my twenty-first birthday. If I was twenty-one, no one could tell me what I can or cannot do, because I would be living all by myself," she thought, looking down at her plate of food. Vesta sat down at the kitchen table.

"Are you going to be all right?" she asked Willa.

"Yes, thanks for asking," Willa responded.

"You know, this could be good news—maybe things around the house will be a lot better now," she added.

"You don't know what you're talking about; you have no idea of what goes on in that house. I live there not you; don't try to make things look brighter," she wanted to lash out, but she kept it all inside. Willa and Vesta ate their breakfast in silence, while Willa never lifted her head so Vesta couldn't see her tears. This is not the first breakfast when the two of them sat in silence, so it wasn't as uncomfortable to them as it would be to most people. They finished eating breakfast.

"I'll wash the dishes, Vesta, so you can get dressed and make your bed," Willa offered.

"Okay, I appreciate the offer," Vesta said, and then turned around and left.

Willa cleared the table and cleaned the stove, then washed, rinsed, dried and put away the dishes. When Willa finished, she went to the back porch to the cleaning closet to get the vacuum cleaner. Jacob was peeking in the back screen door. Her eyes lit up. This is the best birthday gift she could have. "Jason came to get me. I never have to go home again," she thought.

"Hi," he said.

"Hi, what happened to you?" Willa asked him.

"I can't explain right now. I don't want Vesta to come out and find me here. I just wanted to come and say good-bye. I am leaving for Alaska. I heard there are lots of opportunities out there. Don't think that because I'm gone, I am not with you. I will try to write, but your mom will probably just tear up the letters and throw them away," he said.

Willa couldn't believe what she was hearing. It didn't seem real—like it was all a blur and just like a dream.

"Jacob, can I come with you? Please," she begged.

The tears started to flow.

"I can go to school, then after school I can get a job to help with the bills. I am going to college. I won't miss any school. I can keep the house clean for you. Please, Jacob, take me with you, Daddy, please," she pleaded with him.

"I don't think so, Princess. You belong at home with your mom. Maybe with me gone, you will get treated with the respect you deserve," he said.

He had tears in his eyes. Jacob hugged Willa and then gave her a kiss. Then he turned around and left.

As he was leaving, Willa yelled, "I love you, Jacob."

But she didn't think he heard her. "Today has to be the worse day of my life. I have had some pretty horrible days in my life, but this one tops them all. I wish I were dead," she thought, as she sat on the floor of the back porch.

Willa was sobbing so much that she couldn't see anything. She tried taking the vacuum cleaner out of the closet. It had always been so easy to do, but today she didn't have the strength to lift it. She gave up, and fell to her knees, putting her face in her hands and crying harder than she ever cried before. The tears and the sobs wouldn't stop. "It's true," she thought. "I am all alone now, and it is just me." Vesta came in to see what all the noise was about.

"What's wrong?"

She grabbed Willa and held her in her arms. "It's going to be all right, believe me," Vesta said while drying off the tears from Willa's face. "Why don't you go sit down in the living room and forget the chores. The house is clean. It gets cleaned every day and there is no one around to mess it up," Vesta told her.

Willa got up and made her trek to the living room in a daze. She was numb feeling like all of the events of this awful morning were a scene in a movie—like nothing is real.

"God, this is Willa. I want to come home to you now. Please God, take me to be with you. I can't take this life anymore. The pain has become too much for me to handle all alone," Willa prayed silently.

Vesta brought her a glass of water and a couple of aspirins.

"Here, take these, you will be in need of them after you are done with all the crying. I know what it's like to cry that hard. You will get a tremendous headache afterward," she explained, trying to console Willa.

Willa did appreciate what Vesta was trying to do for her, but she just wanted to be alone—to be by herself so she could feel sorry for herself. She took the glass of water and the two aspirins from her hand. She swallowed the pills, feeling them get stuck in her throat, making her drink more water than she could handle.

"Thank you, Vesta," Willa said.

Then she got up to take the glass to the kitchen sink.

"No, you lay down and get some rest. You are going to need it," Vesta ordered.

Willa laid down on the couch and cried herself to sleep.

Everything in the room is spinning; it all becomes a blur because she is spinning so fast. "Where am I?" She cannot make out anything—it is all so blurry, "How did I get here?" she thinks. The spinning starts to slow down and she could see things more clearly. She is in a large concrete room. There is no furniture anywhere. She can see large windows on one side of the room, but there are no doors. Suddenly there are people in the room where she is. "How did they get here?" she wonders. She starts to yell. "Somebody, help me. Please get me down from here." She is now laying on a big wheel. She looks at the people and knows she is too high to jump off. There is no ground underneath the wheel. Her heart starts to race. She can feel the flow of adrenaline, and she is getting scared. She can hear the sound of her heart beating in her ears. It sounds like people are marching inside. She can feel the pulsating beat throughout her body. "Help me, someone," she yells. No one is listening. There are people outside of the windows and she can hear them yelling, "We are here to save you, Lilith. We will try to get you down," they tell her. "Please hurry, the wheel is getting higher. It looks like it will smash me between it and the ceiling. Please hurry," Willa said frantically. She can see them hitting the windows with rocks and other objects. Nothing seems to be able to break the glass. Now suddenly there is no glass. The windows and the people have disappeared, but she can feel the warm air coming in from where the windows were. She can still hear the voices of the people, but no one is there. "Somebody, help me, save me, please. Help me get off of this wheel," she cries out. Then a man appears. He is standing next to the wheel.

"Hi, Lilith, are you surprised to see me?" he asked her.

"I don't know who you are," Willa cried. "I am not who you think I am," she added.

"Don't think you are clever, Lilith. The soul never lies. I know that soul. I can smell it. You can't fool me. That soul belongs to me, remember? I am here to claim what is mine. There is no one who can help you now. Go ahead and scream all you want," he added, and then he disappeared.

"Who is Lilith? Why does he think I am her? He wants to take my soul. What does he plan to do with it?" She was terrified.

She screamed out, "God, help me. Please come to me. Please save me from this place."

Then she hears the voice of the man, "Yell as loud as you want. There is no one who can save you now. Once you fall off of that wheel, your soul is mine. I have waited a long time for this," he said laughing.

The wheel started spinning faster, Willa tried to hold onto something, anything, but there was nothing to hold onto and the wheel was to big to reach either end of it. She closed her eyes. She is too terrified to see what is going to happen to her next. She can feel herself sliding off the wheel as it turns.

"I love you, father in heaven," she shouts, as she feels herself sliding off the wheel.

Her throat is so dry it feels like the warm wind is going through it and into her body. Her head is numb.

"I can't think anymore," she cried.

She could feel herself at the edge of the wheel ready to fall into the hole beneath it. She jumped up, and found herself sitting on the couch where she had fallen asleep. She was sweating, her throat was dry, and her heart was beating fast. She tried to collect her feelings. "Oh, God, the nightmares are back," she thought.

Willa can hear Vesta talking to someone on the phone, so she decided not to disturb her because it was only a dream—a dream that seemed so real, but it was not real. Willa got up off the couch and went to the bathroom. As she went into the bathroom, she didn't notice that the closet door was slightly opened. She went straight to the toilet. When she finished, she went to the sink to wash up. She splashed some water on her face so she could wake up out of that nightmare, because she couldn't stop thinking about it. She grabbed a towel and dried her face; she still had the towel in her hand and on her face when she was facing the closet. She opened her eyes.

"OH, GOD!"

There they were—all of the monsters and demons that had jumped out into the hallway to get her. They have her trapped in the bathroom. Her heart went to her throat. Her head started spinning, and she was finding it hard to breathe. She could feel her consciousness leaving her. She no longer had any feeling in her body—it's all gone. "I am going to die," she thought, and then she fainted. Everything got completely dark. The only thing she could feel was the beating of her heart, which seemed to be slowing down. Her heard got numb, and her entire being was numb.

"I pray you get my soul, Lord," were the last words she remembered saying.

Everything disappeared. She was gone—no dreams, no thoughts; there was nothing—only total silence and darkness.

Willa opened her eyes and a bright light was shining in them. She heard noise in the background, but she couldn't make out what it was. She was lying in a bed covered with a white sheet, and there were machines beeping. Tubes were coming from her body and there was a mask on her face. The walls in the room where she woke up were all white except for the sink on the counter. "Where am I?" she thought, looking around at the room and the tubes coming from her body to the machine or visa versa. It looks and smells like a hospital. "How did I get here?" she thought.

"Is anybody here?" she shouted, hoping to get someone's attention.

"She's awake!"

She heard the sound of Grandpa's voice.

"She is going to make it. She isn't going to die," he was crying.

He ran into the room where Willa was, and put his arms around her and sobbed.

"I love you, Princess. I don't know what I would do if I lost you," he cried.

"How did I get here?" Willa asked.

"Vesta was cleaning out the bathroom closet when the phone rang. She went to answer it, and you stumbled across the Halloween costumes she was using to scare you with all of these years. She was going to throw them away," he explained. "Oh, honey, I am so glad you are alive. I prayed to God, I didn't want to lose you," he said still crying.

The doctor came in, and said, "You gave everyone a scare, little one. When you were brought in, we thought you were not going to make it. You had what we call a cardiac arrest. You might be able to understand it more if I called it a heart attack. You are very strong and persistent," he said. "Okay, I have to ask you if you know what date it is today?" he asked, waiting for Willa to answer.

"Today is July 3, and it's my twelfth birthday," Willa told him.

"No, honey, I'm afraid that was three days ago," he explained. "Next question, but you already answered it, I was going to ask you how old you are," he said with a laugh. "Here's a good one for you. Since you passed the questions test, how would you like to go home tomorrow?" he asked.

"Why can't I go home today?" Willa asked instead of answering his question.

"We have to keep you at least one more day for observation. We have to make sure you are strong enough to get out of the bed. You haven't eaten real food for three days and you are too weak right now. I bet you are starving?" he said.

"Yea, I do feel weak and hungry," she told him.

"We will start you on broth and jello. We don't want you eating solid food quite yet," he explained.

"Okay, I like soup and jello anyway," she told him.

"If all goes well, you can go home tomorrow," he said.

Then he wrote something down on the chart and left.

Willa turned her head and looked at Grandpa, "Are you the only one here?" she asked.

"Yes, I have been sleeping in the hallway waiting for you to wake up," he said. "I am going to leave for a little while," he said. "I need to go home and get cleaned up," he added.

"Yea, you do," Willa thought. She had never seen Grandpa with stubble on his face before.

"I also want to tell everybody that you are okay and you chose between us and God, and you decided to stay with us," he started crying again. "I love you, Princess. I will be back as soon as I get cleaned up, I promise," he said holding onto her.

Then he turned and went out of the room, closing the door behind him. "Vesta was all of my demons and monsters? She is the one who was scaring me all that time? Why does she hate me so much? I have told her numerous times that I love her. Every time I had an episode with something, she was always there afterward to comfort me, and tell me, 'There are no demons.' She would sometimes hold me. I can't believe it. It's not at all over with. I am still having the nightmares." Her thoughts were reeling in her head.

About the Author

Cherie Lee

I am 51 years old, the mother of 6 + 4, grandmother of 21 plus 2 on the way. I enjoy life, family and friends. I work as a cashier and love my job because it is interesting to I meet so many different people on a daily basis and to make friends with the regulars. I love the outdoors, living in Colorado allows me to find beauty all around me, the mountains are an awesome sight to see every day. I have too many hobbies to list because I always find something new that I want to do or try.

www.ingramcontent.com/pod-product-compliance
Lightning Source LLC
Chambersburg PA
CBHW021559280526
45784CB00001BA/422